Beyond The Crack Generation:

Surviving A Trauma Organized Culture

By K-Rahn Vallatine

D0885514

INNER SUN

Published by Inner Sun Inc.

545 N. Rimsdale Ave, Suite 1716

Covina, California 91722, USA

Copyright © 2018 by K-Rahn Vallatine

ISBN: 978-0-9916382-5-3

BOOK COVER DESIGN BY:

Virtually Possible Designs

&

K-Rahn Vallatine

While the author has made every effort to provide accurate internet addresses at the time of publication, neither the publisher nor the author assumes any responsibility for errors, or for changes that occur after publication. Further, the publisher does not have any control over and does not assume any responsibility for author or third-party websites or their content.

BEYOND THE CRACK GENERATION

THE SOULS OF CRACK SMOKE

*Our uncles were
crack addicts*

*Our aunties were
strawberries*

*Our grandfathers
were players*

*Our grandmothers
were hustlers*

*Our fathers were
missing*

*Our mothers were
alone*

*Our police were slave
catchers*

*Our employers were
crack dealers*

*Our teachers were
scared*

*Our heroes were
rappers*

*Our pastors were
underqualified*

*Our legal system was
our enemy*

*Our girlfriends were
bitches*

*Our homies were
niggas*

*Our ambitions were
illusions*

*Our education was
irrelevant*

*Our entertainment
was destructive*

*Our leaders were
dead*

Our path was cloudy

Our odds were slim

Our homes were broken

Our community was divided

Our streets were war zones

Our hearts were angry

Our struggle was ignored

Our options were few

Our GOD was quiet

Our secret was fear

Our sisters were scandalous

Our brothers were ruthless

Our elders were judgmental

Our war was misplaced

Our escape was money

Our money was lacking

Our savior was compromised

Our dysfunction was normal

BUT...

Our Faith is Strong

Our Story is Awesome

Our Resilience is Royal

Our Children are Loved

Our Hopes are High

Our Destiny is Great

Our Plan is Developing

We Are ... The Souls of Crack Smoke

Table of Contents

Introduction

I have had many eye-opening interactions with young people in my years of experience working with them. Many of these moments gave me a heartfelt education, beyond academics, that has shaped my perspectives and molded my approach towards youth engagement.

Experiences of working with young men, heavily gang- and drug–impacted, who sincerely aspire to going to prison one day, to follow in the footsteps of their fathers, uncles and grandfathers, taught me to be less judgmental and that family legacy comes in many forms, whether I personally agree or not. I have learned from teenage girls who have been sexually exploited through prostitution since the age of 12 after being molested by trusted adults and then outcasted by their own household for speaking up that there is often much more to a person's story than what is seen on the surface. I have learned from one incarcerated young man, whose biggest dream is to one night have a family dinner, at a dinner table, with his mom and family, whom he lives with that one can be surrounded by loved ones and still be lonely.

However, one of the most pivotal moments I have learned from doing this work was when I was part of a panel of speakers at a high school in south Los Angeles.

The three other panelists were a bit older than me. One gentleman was in his 40s, one in his 50s and one in his 60s. After we spoke, as the four of us walked through the high school hallway during passing period, a young lady around 15 years old stopped us and asked one of the gentlemen a question that still replays in my head. She asked him, "How are you old?"

Let that sink in for just a moment. The question wasn't "How old are you?" but rather, interestingly, "*How* are you old?" I talk more about this story later in this book. But that encounter, and the sincerity of that question, drove the point home for me that many of our youth need an education that extends beyond just reading, writing, and arithmetic.

In his American literary classic, *Souls of Black Folk,* W.E.B. Du Bois eloquently described the *twoness* of the African American experience. Namely, that being both American and Black encroaches upon us "...two thoughts, two unreconciled strivings; two warring ideals in one dark body..."

I'm sure if Dr. Du Bois could have expounded on his prophetic analysis, he would have also warned us about the ravaging *threeness* that would creep into and haunt the Black community, specifically, the crack cocaine-cultured children of the 1970s and 1980s. He would have told us that jobs would begin to disappear as South American cocaine and Eastern European machine guns would begin to mysteriously appear in urban communities, and that this would result in the evolution of a third personality in the Black community – a personality of culturally accepted and even celebrated psychopathy that internally isolates the individual from the greater society around him.

This third personality rebels against the established social etiquette as well as the hypocrisy of mainstream society, while inwardly seeking to obtain the spoils and wealth this mainstream society has to offer. It is a personality that outwardly takes pride in cultural and ethnic uniqueness of being Black, while inwardly is shamed by the feelings of cultural insecurity and social exclusion. Du Bois would have told us of a personality that makes the souls of Black folk feel both unity and enmity, loyalty and distrust, and support and competition toward others who share this same personality. He would have told us about the effects of trauma, community trauma and the evolution of "trauma organized culture."

In discussions of education and youth engagement, the havoc the crack cocaine epidemic brought to inner cities, and to American society as a whole, has been greatly underemphasized. Quietly behind the stories of drug addiction and family destruction, the heart-wrenching statistics of mass incarceration, and the high numbers of chemically imbalanced babies born addicted to a narcotic they never chose for themselves, stands another compelling story. It is the story of reversed economic and social progress, a tale of inverted generational rankings and the narrative of communal bastardization.

Though many of us were not crack dealers, the soundtrack to our formative preteen and teenage years was filled with "crack rock" Hip Hop anthems widely distributed by mega media corporations. We fell in love with multimillion dollar budgeted, urban crack street tales projected on the silver screen. And we saw all of these exaggerated holograms of

3

entertainment play out daily in the real world around us. With little in place to counteract the real life traumas we experienced in our neighborhoods and the "Dope-Boy" media glorification of the 90s, the paradigms for many of us born in the Hip Hop generation (1970s and 1980s) became skewed. Inflicting violence upon our peers became a tolerated standard and was sometimes even considered a fun way to carry out "community politics." Disrespecting and emotionally abusing young ladies became normal courtship behavior. Preying on the sicknesses and addictions of others for financial gain became an economic way of life.

Within these skewed paradigms, the *threeness* of the African American experience developed. First, as *Americans,* we simply wanted to live in peace within our country and enjoy the American Dream we had heard so much about. Second, as *Black* Americans, we understood America's history of contempt towards us since its inception and that we must continue to fight against its racist ways in order to obtain peace. And third, as children of the crack cocaine culture, we found ourselves standing in the midst of an internal civil war within our own American sub-culture that was fueled by hatred, confusion, desperation and miseducation as we witnessed our peers making a living off of the downfall and death of others. We rejected mainstream acceptance while warring against our own common kinsmen who shared our same struggles. Our environment kept us dying in the midst of our attempt to live.

Three warring ideals in one dark body.

In this book, I offer my first-hand experience as a jump-board starting point to discuss not only community challenges related to culture, paradigm and socio-economics, but also practical solutions that I have already implemented to help our youth heal and recover. *Beyond the Crack Generation* is somewhat of a memoir of a pivotal generation that is searching to discover its own greatness and create a new normal, while at the same time trying to figure out how it was ever lost in the first place.

With that endeavor in mind, *Beyond the Crack Generation* is specifically for anyone who is passionate for community work, violence intervention, urban education or youth engagement. It is also for anyone who has endured or wants insight into the context of those who have endured, the many challenges of living in urban America and is seeking to heal. In attempting to offer social-emotional support to our youth, it is important to have an understanding of the emotional responses they often have to their social experience. This is a book that first points to understanding the sources of problematic symptoms of society, and then offers a remedy.

I. It's Bigger Than Hip Hop

You understand our mindset?
You understand this bomb threat?
Understand 20 years later we got a complex?
Understand traumatized as kids but ain't cried yet
I'm trying to give you content to put things in context

K-Rahn (A Children's Story)

I remember being seven or eight years old, playing on Friday and Saturday nights with my cousins, Joseph and Danielle, in Joseph's room. One of our favorite games was "The Blob," based on the 1988 remake of the horror movie classic. Using our childhood imagination, we would take turns covering ourselves with a blanket and then crawling around the room chasing the others, hoping to catch them by the leg and drag them under the blanket. As each person got caught, the "blob" would of course get bigger, stronger and scarier.

As we ran around frantically trying to escape the dreaded blob, we could feel deep bass vibrations coming through the wall between Joseph's room and his older brother Dontae's. Dontae would stand behind his turntable set mixing Marley Marl and the Juice Crew's song, "The Symphony," with Eazy E's latest single, "Eazy Duz It." That small bedroom felt like a huge gymnasium in those days.

Whenever we would poke our heads out of Joseph's room to go the bathroom or get water, we'd walk through the house hearing our moms and aunties laughing, joking and partying loudly in the living room. I used to love the festive sounds of drinks pouring, glasses clinking, and women laughing as Denise LaSalle's songs, "Down Home Blues" and "Girlfriend, Your Husband's Cheating on Us," played in the background.

This was a great time in my childhood, the late 1980s in Pasadena, California. At this point in life, my cousins and I were not aware of the growing social treacheries taking place in the society around us. We only had dim glimpses that there was a real life socio-economic "Blob" lurking through urban communities all across the country, quietly chasing and capturing young people of color. But unlike the blob of our childhood game, this Blob did not reach for the legs of its victims but reached instead for the lives, freedom and sanity of children who only wanted what everyone else around them wanted: the American Dream.

Who knew that, just like the imaginary monster my cousins and I pretended to be, this societal Blob would keep growing bigger and stronger with each new "recruit" it captured into its lifestyle, making resistance to its way of thinking more and more difficult to resist with each new conversion? Who knew that this monster would continue to haunt our community decades later, even to this day? This Blob is not made of a gelatinous substance like the monster in the movie, nor can it be covered with a simple blanket like in our child's play. No. This Blob is much more deadly. It is made up of a potentially lethal concoction of desperation, manufactured false self-imagery, destructive value systems, oppression, miseducation and lack of opportunity and hope. It is a monster that often goes unrecognized and has yet to be conquered.

Culture Often Dictates Morality

"Culture" can be defined as the social way of life for a specific group of people. It consists of the behaviors, beliefs, values, style of expression, language and symbols that a group of people accept as their defining norm. Of these elements, I must state that the most defining factor of any culture is the set of *values* that culture upholds. While style of expression, such as fashion or slang, may vary among the various members of the culture and continuously change over time, it is a culture's longstanding value system more than any other factor that determines whether you're "in" or "out."

A value system is a set of moral codes that determine what is right and what is wrong within a community or segment of society. It is also the key factor that distinguishes how both success and failure is defined. Although a society's morality is often thought to dictate its culture, what's becoming clearer with each new generation is that a society's dominating culture dictates morality. In society, the standards of right and wrong seem to be ever changing and evolving with time. Many of the customs and traditions that were upheld as normal or even godly many generations ago, such as chattel slavery, are now frowned upon by modern society as wrong. Conversely, practices that were once generally frowned upon by the masses and considered immoral only a few years ago, such as homosexuality, are now embraced and even legally protected. The culture of a few influential people usually will, in time and with persistence, shape and mold the morality of the masses. It would seem, therefore, that morality is subjective and, as such, is heavily influenced by the culture it is set in.

This is extremely important to understand when considering the work of human services on any level, in any arena. The idea of right and wrong is very heavily influenced by the cultural norms of the environment. To illustrate this point, I offer a brief example:

> *Two ten-year-old female students attend two different elementary schools within two different communities where they respectively live. Student A, let's call her Jessica, lives in a community in which she and her parent(s) feel well supported. Parents in general are very active in the school and are trusting and supportive of school staff. Neighborhood residents are cordial and look out for one another, and the police are friendly to local citizens. This community is full of homebuyers and professionals who are actively concerned with property value, higher education*

achievement and long-term wealth building.

Student B, let's call her Jackie, lives in a community in which she and her parent(s) feel unsupported. Parents are not very active in the school and are not trusting or supportive of school staff. Neighborhood residents are often hostile towards each other and even violent. Police are adversarial towards local citizens, and citizens, in turn, are adversarial towards law enforcement. This community is full of low-income and/or unemployed renters who are mostly concerned with surviving day to day, respect and reputation amongst peers, and immediate personal financial gain.

While in their respective schools one day, both Jessica and Jackie each are confronted by another student who slaps her in the face in front of their classmates.

Let's consider how Jessica, Student A, will typically respond versus Jackie, Student B.

Generally speaking, since Jessica feels supported by her community, she will most likely cry and go and tell a teacher about being assaulted by the other student. She cries because she feels emotional supported by her peers. She feels safe to cry in her environment. She tells the teacher because she trusts that the teacher will properly handle the situation justly. As a result, Jessica will continue on with her day without further incident. Though she may be upset that she was slapped, she is relieved that a fair and honest teacher is there to vindicate her and resolve the issue. Her parents taught her that fighting is not the solution and telling someone in authority about such problems is definitely the best way to address the situation. Jessica and probably most all of her peers have been taught this way and are very concerned about not getting in trouble at school.

In contrast, again speaking generally, since ten-year-old Jackie feels unsupported by her community, she will most likely have a very different experience after being assaulted by the other student. She probably will not cry. Not because she is naturally less emotional that than Jessica. No, she will not cry because she does not feel emotionally supported by her peers. She does not feel safe to cry in her environment. The chances of her going to tell her teacher are very slim. Instead, she will almost immediately hit the other student back and engage in a fist fight. She feels isolated from her teachers and authority figures because she does not trust they will handle the situation properly. Jackie is not a violent or angry child, but she was taught by her mother that "If someone puts their hands on you, you hit them back and hit them back harder to make sure they never put their hands on you again."

Furthermore, Jackie is taught by her community that she is not to be a "tattle-tale." In her community, a tattle-tale is a "snitch," and as she gets older, she will also learn that "snitches get stitches" or, and depending on the severity of the situation, "stitches get ditches." In other words, if a victim tells some authority that another community member has committed an infraction, the victim will be physically hurt, ridiculed by their community and maybe even killed.

But not only has Jackie's mother told her that "If someone hits you, you better hit them back harder," she has also warned her that "If you don't hit them back, when you come home you'll have deal with me! And don't worry about getting in trouble with your *little* teachers. I will deal with them." Ten-year old Jackie may not even want to fight, but according to the culture in which she is being "nurtured," she feels she has to because her mother will be angry with her if she doesn't. Plus, if she doesn't, her schoolmates will tease her, call her names and bully her. And the student who hit her will come for her again. Worst of all, if she doesn't fight back, she will have a reputation in her community of being weak or a "punk" – a label that will follow her in her community throughout her life until she proves otherwise. Jackie will become prey to the violent impulses of her peers.

So, what does Jackie do? She fights against her own will.

Is Jackie's mother a bad parent for teaching her young child to respond to violence with violence? Not necessarily. Her mother's focus is probably not on teaching her daughter to be violent but on teaching her how not to be a victim. Jackie's mother knows very well of the harsh social reality her daughter is growing up into and understands that, as her mother, she must somehow prepare Jackie to be a survivor. She therefore consciously equips her daughter with the perspectives and skills she as a mom has to offer and that she feels Jackie will need for the immediate world she has begun to face.

Ok. So, Jackie wins the fist fight, and beats up the other student.

From a youth engagement viewpoint, if the culture in which Jackie is being nurtured is not taken into consideration and somewhat understood by her school administration, her perspective will be overlooked, and she will be thoughtlessly punished for fighting and maybe even labeled as "bad," "angry" or "a trouble-maker." Jackie will be suspended from school and left on her own to work through feeling confused, misunderstood, unfairly treated and un-vindicated by the authority figures in her school. This will lead to further isolation and distrust of school authority that will develop into an underlying adversarial relationship between Jackie, her school and authority figures as she wrestles with questions in her mind. "Why am I the one in trouble? I was just doing what my mother told me to do, so why am I being punished? She hit me first and all I did was what I was supposed to do. Don't they understand what would happen if I didn't fight her?"

In such a scenario, the concept of a clear right and wrong – of morality – begins to blur. Is it wrong for an individual to hit and be violent? Depends on whom you ask and in what setting. In preschool where the culture is greatly influenced by Sesame Street-type characters and the immediate culture is safe and supportive, yes, hitting could be quickly and easily identified as wrong. In elementary school and up, when the culture is greatly influenced by the code of the streets and the surrounding environment is generally unsupportive and sometimes even warlike, then the answer may be no. In the latter setting, one ironically learns that it is actually wrong to be nonviolent, that it is wrong to not hit back.

Furthermore, if Jessica, from community A, instead decided to fight the girl who slapped her and beats the girl up but as a result gets suspended for two days, in her mind, did she "win" or "lose?"

Answer? She lost. She has been taught that staying out of trouble in school is winning and much more important than reputation.

If Jackie wins the fist fight but as a result gets suspended for five days, in her mind did she "win" or "lose?"

Answer? She won. She has been taught to never let anyone disrespect you under no circumstance. So indirectly respect from peers is winning and much more important than getting in trouble at school.

Of course, these are generalizations to make a point: Culture defines what it means to win or lose, to succeed or fail.

Thankfully, educational institutions do exist that seek to serve communities challenged with unsupportive and contentious norms. Such settings recognize the fact that establishing a healthy culture for students that is contrary to their current surrounding environment is imperative, and they implement corresponding policies and practices that allow the staff, the students and the parents to feel physically and emotionally safe.

This concerted effort aligns with the trauma informed approach to community service. Going back to Student B, Jackie, to help her smoothly transition from feeling unsafe in her community to a feeling of security and support, the institution must first establish a sense of trust. Since in this community, Jackie is not the exception but the norm, disciplinary decisions must be executed with transparency, leaving no question as to why the process is unfolding the way it is.

Specifically, the disciplinary process must be explained in way that Jackie and her parents clearly understand why she is receiving the consequence she is receiving. There has to be some form of conversation and mediation that levels the power differences between school staff and Jackie, so that

Jackie can truly be heard, her voice empowered, and her feelings validated.

So, in Jackie's scenario, several things must be made clear to her. She must understand that violence is totally unacceptable in the school's culture, but also that it will be addressed equally, consistently and fairly. She must understand that her consequence is a result of participating in school violence and not for winning the fight. She needs to see that even though she beat the girl up, it is understood that her actions were in response to being attacked and that therefore, up to a point in the engagement with the other student, she was the victim and the other student will also receive a consequence for participating in violence. Jackie must also be made to recognize that during the fight, she went from victim to attacker, engaging in combat that went beyond self-defense. This too must be addressed.

An approach to crime that is gaining great momentum is the theory of "restorative justice." Restorative justice seeks to address the harm that wrongdoing causes to people, relationships and community. A main component of the process is gathering the involved and willing parties together to discuss both the harm and the resolution to a conflict with the goal of achieving positive transformation in the relationship.

Remember, not only were Jackie and her attacker affected by the altercation. Other students who witnessed the girl slap Jackie and Jackie beat her up were also affected, as were parents who heard about it and the way it was handled. If such a situation is not handled properly, students and parents will have a continued perception that the school environment is unsafe, unfair, or both. However, with consistency, transparency and fairness, the culture of the school can be transformed into one of safety and trustworthiness. This, in turn, will positively influence and develop a healthy concept of wrong and right – morality – in the environment.

"This rap thang always was my plan A, dreaming of exchanging multimillion dollar handshakes"

I've been a rap fan since the age of five. No exaggeration. My older cousin Dontae, whose music used to vibrate the walls of his brother's room, was a die-hard Hip Hop fan and mixtape DJ. As a young child, even though I went to my cousin's house to play with Joseph, who was my age, I often found myself spending a lot of time in Dontae's room, who was nine years older than me. He had crates and crates full of rap albums and spun Hip Hop cuts all day long. He probably literally had every single rap album out during that time. I would just sit quietly in his room or outside his room in the hallway listening to the music. I loved it. As he played song after song, I would ask him, "Who is that you're playing? What's the name of that song?" Even though he would be clearly annoyed, song after song, he would tell me the answer.

I received my first rap record around age four or five. It was the Fat Boys' 1985 single "Chillin' with the Refrigerator," a tribute to the Chicago Bears' running back, William "The Refrigerator" Perry. I'm not really sure how I got it. It wasn't the best song, but it was a start to get me deeper into Hip Hop culture.

Then *it* happened. Shortly after owning that first single, I sat in Dontae's room as he played LL Cool J's debut album, *Radio*. This was definitely the

17

best music I had ever heard in my short life. I mean, George Clinton's "Atomic Dog" was great. And I'll admit, at age five I could even get down with Wham's "Wake Me Up Before You Go-Go." But this LL guy was raw, angry, confident and so *cool*. I had to have it. So, of course, I immediately asked my cousin, "Who is that?" He show me the album cover and said, "This is LL Cool J." That same night I asked my mom if she would buy it for me and, thankfully, she said yes! About a week later, I had it!

Once I got that cassette tape, at five years old, I thought I had found my life's calling. I was put on Earth to be a rapper! I remember playing LL's song, "I Can't Live Without My Radio," in front of my Auntie Clarretta and performing it like it was *my* song – with her son, Joseph, and her granddaughter, Danielle, as my backup singers. "*My radio believe me I like it loud. I'm the man with the box that can rock the crowd...*"

As the years 1986 and 1987 passed by, I continued to sit in cousin Dontae's room listening to music and asking him, "Who is that?" I even asked him to make me a mixtape full of rap songs. He would always answer my questions and eventually made me that mixtape, after months of my begging. I listened to this cassette tape over and over, every day. Then 1988 came. By now I was listening to L.A.'s Hip Hop radio station, 1580 KDAY, on AM radio and was becoming very familiar on my own with who was who in the rap game. If I remember correctly, it was in this year that I got Big Daddy Kane's cassette tape, "Long Live the Kane," Biz Markie's "Goin' Off" and Salt N Pepa's "A Salt with a Deadly Pepa." This was a golden year in Hip Hop for me.

Then one day I was with Dontae after his high school basketball practice and we got a ride home with one of his friends. All I remember about this guy was that he was short and had a Jheri curl. I got into the back seat of his hatchback Volkswagen Rabbit, and he and Dontae sat in the front. And then.... they turned up the music.

Who would have known this would be a turning point for me, the beginning of a forever paradigm shift in my psyche?

As Dontae's friend began to drive, I heard the prophetic words, "You are now about to witness the strength of street knowledge," echo through the subwoofers behind me. Then came a hypnotic beat like I had never heard before. And then a voice – more raw, more angry, more confident, more cool and more relatable than any voice I had ever heard before in music: *"Straight outta Compton, crazy muthafucka named Ice Cube, from a gang called niggaz with attitude."*

I was about eight or nine years old and could not believe what my young ears were hearing. I had never heard anybody rap like *that*. The lyrics, the rhyme pattern, the unapologetic disregard for political correctness, the skits and sound effects inside the song, the cussing. Listening to the song felt like I was inside of a movie.

We reached Donte's house before the song ended. "Who was that on the song your friend was playing in the car?" I asked Dontae as we walked to his front door. "That was N.W.A." Dontae replied. I thought to myself, "Okay! I gotta remember those letters! N-W-A." I hadn't felt this excited about music since I had heard LL Cool J's debut album a few years back. I most definitely had to have this tape.

I later found out N.W.A. was an acronym that stood for "Niggas With Attitude." The name expresses the acceptance of the "nigga" title in

19

society, but not the docile caricatures of the past associated with being considered a "nigger." They instead were *niggas*, but with attitude. I would later in life understand this on a deeper level.

Of course, I couldn't ask my mother for this one. Luckily for me, her boyfriend at the time was a sophisticated hustler from South Central Los Angeles named Amir, who always talked about being a "high roller." He had been in our lives for about four years by this time and was a member of the Nation of Islam. He owned a stretch limousine company, wore slacks and button-down shirts daily, and was very cool and street smart. I had to get that N.W.A. tape and I knew Amir was the person to ask. I asked him if he would take me to buy a cassette tape and he said he would. "Yes!" I thought. "I'm half way there!"

A few days later, Amir and my mother took me to a mom-and-pop record store in Los Angeles. I immediately asked the sales guy, "Where is your rap section?" As he pointed me in the right direction, I walked away from my mom and Amir towards the rap cassettes and went straight to the "N" section. There it was! They had two N.W.A. cassettes, *N.W.A. and the Posse* and *Straight Outta Compton*. I wasn't sure which one to get, but I remembered that first line of that rap verse I heard: *Straight Outta Compton, crazy muthafucka named Ice Cube.* "It must be the second one," I thought to myself.

I looked at the cassette cover and saw six guys, whose faces I could barely see, standing in a huddle-like circle looking down into the camera. In small red letters in the corner of the cassette cover it said, "Parental discretion is suggested." This was just before the days of the large, black and white "Parental Discretion Is Advised" labels conspicuously stamped on cassette covers or albums that contained explicit language.

I nonchalantly grabbed the N.W.A. cassette, walked to my mom and Amir and told *him* I found the one I wanted. My mom said, "Let me see." "Uh-oh," I thought as I handed her the cassette. "What's this 'N dubbaya A'?" "I don't know," I replied. "They have some songs I like." I looked at her and then looked at Amir. Then, she looked at Amir, and Amir looked at me. "It's OK," he said as he grabbed the cassette out of her hand and took it to the register. "Yes!" I said to myself.

As we walked through the record shop, I felt like I was walking through the tunnel of a spaceship about to enter a portal that leads to another dimension. We stood at the cash register as Amir paid for the cassette and I anxiously waited for Scotty to beam me up! Then Amir handed the Niggas With Attitude, *Straight Outta Compton* cassette to my young eight-year-old hands. The rest is history. I was sonically introduced to the harsh, obscene, vulgar and un-empathetic themes of much of urban reality that characterized the 1980s. Though I was raised in urban environments, my mother did a great job at keeping me sheltered from much of what was going on in the community around me up to this point. My eight-year-old ears would listen to this tape through the headphones of my Walkman day after day.

I listened closely to the anthem that spoke fiercely against law enforcement in response to a police brutality I had never before heard of or witnessed. "*F--- the police*" repeatedly vibrated my eardrums. Raw and extremely explicit narratives about a day in the life of an L.A. gang member -- not necessarily a Blood or a Crip, but in this case a member of the fictional gang N.W.A. – unfolded as I repeatedly heard *"Gangsta! Gangsta! That's what they yellin'!"* I heard obscene, vulgar and exceedingly true-to-life commentary, words that painted a realistic picture of the daily effects of the vicious and brutal crack cocaine epidemic that raged through urban communities all across our country.

I listened as the rappers spoke about the sexual purposes they thought women were "good for" and heard their one-dimensional descriptions of women, that painted them as gold-digging, deceitful manipulators. I heard unapologetic descriptions of men as niggas and women as bitches. Though my mother taught me well and was laying a strong, positive foundation for my life, these songs had a powerful influence. Being so young and having little to no social context to put these lyrics into, it was as if my mind was a semi-blank canvas and the rappers were the painters. I soaked up their message like a damp sponge. I was being taught about much of the world around me through listening to the poetry of these young, post-adolescent entertainers. My paradigm was being molded. As one of the songs stated, *Life ain't nothin' but b's and money.* Some people say music is only entertainment, but for many of us born in my generation, regardless of whether it was right or wrong, rap lyrics were a trusted source for many of our life lessons about manhood, womanhood and life in general.

During this period of my life, I remember at times riding throughout Los Angeles alone in the back of stretch limousines as Amir drove around making his runs and handling his daily affairs. He would raise the partition, leaving me in the comfort of my own privacy, equipped with tinted windows, a car television and, of course, a nice booming sound system. Once the partition was up, I would blast N.W.A.'s album at high volume and have my own private party in solitude, while Amir and his close friend sat in the front seat, riding around, talking and laughing.

Since Amir never said anything about the lyrics I was listening to, I figured everything was all good. Then one day while riding around, my eight-year-old mind thought it was a good idea to begin blasting my N.W.A. tape at high volume prematurely, before Amir raised up the partition. I was playing "F--- the Police!" Amir and his friend laughed And said, "Whoa. They're saying some heavy stuff on that tape you're listening to." Shortly after, he raised the partition and went on with the day as usual without a further word about it.

At home the next morning, I grabbed my Walkman, put on my headphones, pressed the play button and noticed my N.W.A. cassette was not in there. I looked all over my room but couldn't find it. I knew I left it in my Walkman because I had listened to it before I went to sleep the night before. After what felt like endless searching, I asked my mother if she had seen my cassette. She replied "Yes. I put it up." "Put it up? What do you mean?" I asked. "Amir told me about that N dubbaya A you've been playing," she answered. "He told me I need to check out what you're listening to." Needless to say, that was the last I would see of that cassette tape. But the messages received and lessons learned from the music would stay with me for years and decades to come.

II. Bastard Generation

Product of my atmosphere,
Damaged by Crack and beer
moving way past my fears,
we make it look attractive here.
Came here as African,
Chopped down to half a man
It's gonna be a long journey before me,
But I got the wind to rise again.

K-RAHN (SHINING STAR)

N.W.A. and other artists who followed may
have rapped harsh and vulgar lyrics, but they
certainly did not create the harsh and vulgar realities
they rapped about. Sure, once Ice Cube left the
group, N.W.A. focused less on social commentary
and became more pornographic and violent.
However, the fact remains that most of the rap music
coming out all across America at that time was being
created in the midst of drug-infested, gun-polluted,
gang impacted urban war zones that used to be
thriving, community-minded neighborhoods. Much

of the obscene lyrics were simply a reflection of the poor social conditions that were a result of the infamous "Crack Epidemic."

I remember when I was a young child, my mom would drive my cousin Nick and me around Pasadena in her 1980-something Nissan 200SX. Among the people we'd sometimes see along Colorado Boulevard was a homeless man in raggedy clothes and unkempt hair, walking down the sidewalk of the busy street, pushing a shopping cart full of cans and miscellaneous possessions. "There's Randal," my mom would say to Nick. She would then get quiet and fade down memory lane for a moment, and then she'd say, "He used to be so smart ... and so handsome." Randal was her cousin, and he was Nick's father. In a solemn voice, she would then add, "Them drugs..." as we quietly, awkwardly drove past him.

Randal was strung out on crack cocaine. He was an addict. And like many of the countless others who were crack addicted, Randal was invisible. Randal was devalued. Randal was another fallen victim, full of suffocated potential and lost hope, relegated to the label "crackhead."

crack • head - *a person who habitually smokes crack cocaine*

The Crack Epidemic of the 80s was a pivotal time in American history. It shifted culture forever and claimed the lives and legacies of many souls. I therefore have come to view urban American history in terms of "B.C." and "A.D." – or, *Before Crack* and *After Distribution*. In order to accurately analyze and assess what's going on with today's disengaged youth, we must trace the roots of their culture back to this period, because this was a time when families were destroyed, rampant violence raged through urban communities, blatant disparities in drug sentencing became a judicial norm, mass imbalanced incarceration boosted the prison population, community values shifted, and communal generational rankings of authority flipped upside down.

As with most other drugs that come with each generation, I'm told that in the late 1970s and early 1980s, crack cocaine started off as somewhat of a "party drug." It was supposed to be a cheaper version of the more expensive party favorite, powder cocaine. Unfortunately, what early experimenters and fun seekers did not know was that this new, cheaper form of the drug was extremely addictive, and would bring devastation to both their lives and that of their loved ones.

If you've ever experienced life around a person addicted to crack or witnessed the effects crack addiction has on their character, you've noticed that often drastic and unfortunate changes happen over a short period of time. The person may become very desperate, manipulative and unconcerned with the affairs of life around them. Their primary, all-consuming concern throughout the day and night is finding their next *hit*. As kids, we saw many highly respectable urban community heroes all across this nation devolve into dishonorable, despicable outcasts almost overnight.

Two extremely crucial points to mention regarding the Crack Epidemic are:

(1) The psychological addiction to crack cocaine was at times so strong that it caused some mothers to abandon or even sell their children for a single hit of crack, which from what I hear, only offers the addict a five- to 10-minute high. Crack

27

addicts often became zombie-like, a hollow shell of the man or woman they used to be. Contrary to all the "crack head" jokes out there, it is definitely a sad and gruesome sight.

(2) Unlike any other previous drug trade, the crack cocaine business was a child's business. This means that although crack addicts were most often adults, the crack sellers were often children as young 10 years old! And while the 1980s were marked by unprecedented violent drug wars that left urban Black and Brown communities across the nation feeling like a government-abandoned, war-torn, so-called third world country, by the mid-1990s many crack dealers were not the hardcore thugs or "super predators" that some thought them to be. Actually, many were school kids turned drug pushers. School kids with support systems at home.

One huge factor contributing to this unique phenomenon was the fact that there were few if any obstacles for children to enter "the game." Crack cocaine was a drug that was easy to get and practically sold itself. During my early teenage years, I saw several of my peers easily enter the drug trade with no obstacles. In other drug trades, you generally needed the permission and guidance of older dealers before you could fully get in the game. But with crack, there was little to no preliminary protocol or initiation to start selling. The only true prerequisite was that you had to be accepted by the other hustlers in the streets and on the corners.

For my particular childhood peer group, it didn't require a lot of money to get started. A child could literally save their lunch money for a week or two, or cut some grass or recycle some cans, and soon have enough start-up capital to begin their own corner business. Or they could be "fronted," meaning the drug supplier would give the young, new drug dealer some product to sell on consignment and the dealer paid the supplier back once the product was sold.

Here's how it works: A 13-year-old kid (male or female) goes to the local supplier, usually an older kid in his late teens or early 20s who for the most part sells to anyone as long as they have the money. Twenty dollars gets the new dealer $40 worth of crack to sell. Approaching a supplier with the intention to buy crack that the young dealer could sell is similar to the kid having a wholesale license. As a distributor, the new dealer is able to purchase the product at this heavily discounted rate, while the direct consumers – the crack addicts – have to pay the "retail price." The supplier refuses to sell product at the low, discounted rate to "retail customers."

Once the new drug dealer sells his newly purchased inventory, like real life magic – POOF! – he just doubled his money! So then he takes that fresh $40 and buys another "double-up" from his supplier. Yes, he spends $40 and gets $80 worth of *dope*. He then sells that, and now he has an easy $80 in his pocket. He can now either buy an $80 double-up and "hustle" to double all of that money, or he can pocket half and buy another $40 double-up and do it again. Either way, literally in a matter of minutes or hours, depending on his hustle game and corner positioning, he has well more than the $20 he started with.

This was the perfect hustle for the young adolescent with dreams of one day building a street empire like the urban fictional movie heroes Tony Montana from "Scarface" or Nino Brown from "New Jack City." With crack cocaine, a kid could wake up in the morning and start off his day as a poor middle

29

school student with aspirations of one day going to college and becoming a doctor, and literally by the end of the night be transformed into a full-time dope dealer with hundreds of dollars in his pocket. With this virtually instant financial gratification, who needs to waste time going to college?

I must also mention, because the crack business often attracted robbers, or jackers, as well as situations that often led to violent confrontation, though the young dealer had drugs and money in one pocket, inevitably a gun would soon end up in his other pocket. Guns were extremely accessible to teens at this time. Though no one knew how they got there, or even questioned this, young people all across the country knew who to talk to and how to get them. There was always someone in the neighborhood offering to sell a gun.

Now remember, this teenage crack dealer was not necessarily a "bad" kid. He was just a kid who took a chance and seized the unfortunate but readily available opportunity presented to him by the community he was being raised in. His rationale? "The addict is going to buy and smoke crack anyway, so why not get in where I fit in and make money from it?"

With access to guns and a means to make a lot of immediate cash, kids began to lose trust in traditional authority figures to provide for us or protect us. So, we started fending for ourselves. One significant result was that, when crack hit the streets, the generational hierarchy became inverted. The kid selling the dope – and carrying the gun – now had the power, and the crack addicted adults acted as mere children in this teenager's presence.

Take a moment to think about how becoming the authority and power figures of their community affects the psyche of a new generation of children. A

13-year-old crack dealer who once respected his elders, now has learned to have little or no respect for his adult clientele. It was a gruesome and unbelievably tragic sight to see a friend's or neighbor's uncle or auntie, adults we knew and grew up with, now begging a mere child for crack, willing to do literally anything for another hit. Without getting graphic for the purposes of this book, let me stress the word *anything*. These addicts would do whatever that young teenage crack dealer's mind could imagine. Inevitably, the power roles in the community shifted and the kid was now king.

This child now had the product that many adults craved and became fiends for, and he also had the money that many adults who worked 40 hours a week would never earn. Furthermore, because the crack cocaine trade was such a ruthless and violent business, the kid now also had the fear and respect of his community at a level that the upstanding adult would never obtain.

This social setting kind of reminds me of a real-life version of the book, *The Lord of The Flies,* where a group of young boys find themselves on an island with no adults and had to learn to fend for themselves, resorting to violence to survive and to establish a hierarchy of authority.

The Abnormal Norm

I spent half of my high school years living in the Mid-West. Muncie, Indiana, to be specific. Upon the initial word that we were moving, I was devastated. It was the second semester of my ninth-grade year. I was always younger than my classmates and extremely shy, but I was on the JV football team and my popularity was slowly rising. My mother had gotten word that my grandmother was sick, so we had to go check on her, which of course I understood. My mother promised me we would be there for two months to help nurse my grandmother back to health and then we would return back home to California. To our surprise, our planned two-months turned into one year for my mother and two whole years for me.

We arrived in Indiana in the winter of 1993. Snoop Doggy Dog had just released his debut album, *Doggystyle*. With the exception of the Bloods & Crips album, *Bangin' on Wax,* which was released earlier that year, Snoop Doggy Dog and the Death Row Records camp were the first group of artists and executives I had ever seen bring Los Angeles gang affiliations so blatantly to mainstream culture and to the forefront of their music. Artists before this had many gang affiliations that people knew about, and they made underground songs that clearly announced their affiliations, but this was something different.

I held on to that Snoop Dogg tape and played it like it was my West Coast lifeline. It felt like high dosages of this album would help keep me true and connected to my Southern California roots. Indiana was a completely different world to me.

First of all, it was freezing cold. I don't mean freezing like we'd say in sunny Southern California on a rare night when the temperature dropped below 60 degrees. I mean literally *freezing.* I'm talking buying huge bags of salt to pour on your driveway to melt the ice *freezing.* Keeping all your faucets slightly running throughout the night so the water doesn't freeze and bust the pipes *freezing.* Below zero degrees *freezing.* Snow was everywhere.

Still, while the Mid-West looked and felt a lot different than the climate and terrain of California, I quickly realized that my new found teen peer group had much of the same cultural values and social challenges that we had in Los Angeles. The gang culture that was rapped about on the *Doggystyle* album was there – though this was a small town, so of course it differed in the way it was expressed and represented. Guns were there. The misogyny and over-sexualization of young women were there. Poor academic achievement among Black boys was there. And, sadly, the crack epidemic was there. What I thought was going to be a bland and insignificant experience ended up being a crucial and extremely pivotal period in my life.

Muncie was very small, and it seemed we kids had access to everything. I was around age 13 and the Crack Epidemic put almost anything a kid wanted within arms' reach. My mother grew up in this town and would always share with me stories about the tightknit community she was nurtured in. She used to talk endlessly about being a part of social movements and community events and how involved the local church was in community affairs. She talked about brotherhood and sisterhood and how supportive residents in her neighborhood were of each other.

Unfortunately, by the time I reached my teenage years and arrived at the city of her childhood, those days of old had gone up in smoke, morphing into a new kind of culture. As I mentioned before, A.D. (after distribution) looks a lot different than B.C. (before crack). In the summer, the parks were always filled with teenagers playing basketball, shooting dice, smoking weed and having fun. However, all throughout the year, spring, summer, fall, or winter, the corners, mainly among the housing projects, were occupied by teenage crack dealers. Since most of our mothers were usually out working and were not home, many of us hung out freely, going from house to house, having a blast. I'd also spend a lot of my time alone either watching the 70s movie "The Mack," or a bootleg VHS copy of "Menace II Society" on an almost daily basis.

One particularly interesting detail about this community in Muncie that I did not realize until I began reflecting in my recent years as an adult, is that no one I hung out with had a father in the home. I mean, literally, *NO....ONE*. Not one of my homeboys, not one of my homegirls, not one of my girlfriends, not one of my cousins and not me. None of us had fathers present in the home. The only kid I can think of who did have his father in the home, raising him, was a close friend of mine's cousin who I'd see from time to time.

Let's stop and think about that for a moment. We grew up as teenage boys and teenage girls with absolutely no fathers in our homes and seeing no fathers in the homes of almost anyone we knew. At the same time, the culture of gangs and drugs raged through the communities we lived in. And all the while, multimillion dollar corporations were producing, heavily marketing and distributing music that glorified gang and drug culture, reinforcing false senses of manhood and leading to our very destruction.

The reason I emphasize this point is not to highlight this fatherless home dynamic as a rare occurrence to Muncie, but to emphasize the opposite. During the 1980s and 1990s, fatherless homes were a common household dynamic for many young men and women, from neighborhood to neighborhood all across this country. I know the saying goes, "There is nothing new under the sun," but I've yet to learn or read about any previous people since the beginning of human civilization whose social norm was having their children grow up without paternal guidance. Trace back thousands of years, continent to continent, well into the ancient eras of mankind and you still will not find a generation of children who were consistently raised into adulthood without fathers. We very well may be the first "fatherless" generation in the history of man! After speaking to many individuals from my peer group in our adult years, I found that this bizarre dynamic was so common, I was not the only one who failed to notice it in my youth. For many of us, dysfunctional relationships and counter-productive culture were often normalized and accepted as just how things were.

Looking back on dynamics such as this, I must make the point that just because a situation is *common*, we should not necessarily declare it to be *normal, healthy* or *natural*. Common, normal and healthy are not always the same thing.

As a young child, I used to visit Muncie every summer while school was out. I had cousins who lived there. So, once I actually moved there as a teen, I adapted quickly. I immediately began hanging out with my 15-year-old cousin, James. James was a tall, charismatic jokester. He always dressed according to the latest trends and seemed to have every material thing a teenager could want – even a new moped, which was almost like having a car. I thought James was rich. But actually, he and his brother Kevin lived with their grandmother and received a check every month due to the death of their father, my uncle. Their father was murdered, and their mother was unfortunately directly affected by the crack epidemic.

James took me under his wing and introduced me to his clique of six other young men. They were very tight with each other, meeting up every day, hanging out and cracking jokes. Though I had made a few other friends, I began to hang with James and his clique as if I, myself, had grown up with them. They were gang affiliated and were also highly respected in the neighborhood. My bond with them continued to develop over the weeks and months to come.

On one summer weekend night as I was coming home, my mother met me on the porch. "Your friends just left here a few minutes ago looking for you," she said. "Did they say where they were going?" I asked. "Nope." I thought, "Aw. I wonder what they're getting into tonight." This was before cellphones were popular and none of us had pagers at the time. I went into the house, called one of my girlfriends and called it a night. I didn't talk to any of the guys the next day.

A couple days later I found out that the reason a few of them had stopped by my house was to pick me up on their way to a party. Days later I would find out that, though that fateful night may have started with the harmless intent of going to a teenage party and having a good time, it ended tragically, with pain, death and regret.

Five of my seven friends went to the party, got intoxicated and, from what I hear, had a good time. After the party, while walking home through a park, they crossed paths with a lone man. I'm not sure of the details about that encounter. All I know is that the next day the news reported that a man was found beaten and dead in the park from a brain injury. Over the next few days I saw five of my friends get arrested, one by one, in connection to a murder. At this time, I was 14 years old and my friends ranged in age between 15 and 16 years old. The charges against them ranged from voluntary manslaughter to murder, with sentences ranging from 45 to 60 years in prison.

It was incredibly tragic for the victim and his family, who were forced to endure this fatal outcome. It was also extremely unfortunate for these five kids, because I know they had no intent on killing this man. It is unfortunate that these five kids, like many others, were so poorly socialized by the culture and so desensitized to violence through both entertainment and their immediate environment, that at the time they saw little wrong with beating this man. These young teens had a support system at home, and each had a parent that offered them sound moral guidance. Yet and still, such a tragic and disastrous turn of events.

How could this be?

Was it the suppressed anger that many young boys of color all across this country carry within them daily, a tormenting "thorn in the flesh" like the one stuck in the biblical Apostle Paul's side? Was it connected to the reality that most urban youth are not given permission by their environments to truly feel and express any emotion other than anger? Does such recklessness have anything to do with the lack of purpose and the lack of self-worth felt by so many young people? Or was it the consistent hunger and quest for authentic manhood that many of us faced as adolescents?

Maybe destructive behaviors such as this are directly connected to the traumas, complex traumas and the trauma-organized culture that many of my generation had to endure while growing up in our respective urban communities. Unfortunately, many of my teenage peers made their mistakes before trauma-informed research, such as Sandra Bloom's Sanctuary Model and Kaiser Permanente's Adverse Childhood Experience Study (ACES), became well known and nationally supported. My peer group is the generation that former first lady Hillary Clinton

37

once made reference to in a speech delivered at Keene State College and recorded by C-SPAN on January 25, 1996, stating that "they are often the kinds of kids that are called 'super predators' – no conscience, no empathy." Since making this statement, the former Secretary of State has expressed that she shouldn't have used those words and wouldn't use them today [2016]. However, judging by the lack of youth programs at the time, the harsh treatment often received from law enforcement and the abandonment by adults, I'm sure during this period, Mrs. Clinton was not alone in her sentiments about our generation.

The reality is, we were a misguided and abandoned generation of children who were consistently exploited by both corporate and street opportunists for financial gain. We were a generation nurtured in a climate of normalized and celebrated dysfunction. Themes of our destruction were rapped about in chart-topping, #1 *Billboard* songs across the nation. Melodies of our death were danced to and recited throughout pop culture. Real life urban menaces – who once terrorized neighborhoods with violence and criminal acts – became household caricatures, idolized by the masses for their urban tales, "street cred" and striking ability to "keep it real." Prior criminal activity became a rite of passage into the alluring Hip Hop business that we as kids lusted for. In short, we became the *Pop Crack Hip Hop Generation*.

So Much Trouble On My Mind

In February 1996, I moved back to sunny Pasadena, California, to finish high school. Rapper 2Pac had just recently been released from prison and had also just released his double disc CD, *All Eyez on*

Me. It felt like perfect timing. "California Love" was blaring on the airwaves and I was back home, feeling the euphoric Cali love vibe in a major way.

As a teenager, I was highly intelligent, shy yet charismatic, but I placed little value on succeeding in school. I always thought I was going to be a rich and famous rap star. In my mind, high school was just a place to hang out, talk to girls, shoot dice and make money. Ever since I was a little child, my mother consistently sowed into my psyche the importance of entrepreneurship, so I was clear I was not getting a diploma just so I could work for someone else. Like most from my peer group, I had what I thought were bigger and better dreams. Unfortunately, though we knew what we didn't want, outside of entertainment (sports, music and film) many of us were very unclear about what we *did* want – and even more unclear on how to get it.

Returning to California and reminiscing on my two-year stay in Indiana made it clear that the statement by rap group, The Geto Boys, was true: "The World is a Ghetto" (even though the group WAR said it first). I realized even more that though the terrain of Southern California was very different than that of central Indiana, the socio-economic issues of both urban Black communities were in many ways the same. I'm sure much of the normalized dysfunction we witnessed and participated in as teenagers and young adults has caused much emotional and psychological trauma in both my peers and in myself.

Mental health challenges and trauma have often been taboo subjects in much of the urban Black community. The once heavy religious tradition in Black churches influenced many people to believe they could simply pray the mental disorder away. Some thought that speaking to a pastor or minister might be much more effective than talking to a mental health therapist – and if not much more effective, then definitely much more accessible, affordable, and respectable. Considering the extended history of blatant oppression and struggle that have plagued Blacks in the United States – from the enslaved African, to the emancipated Negro, to the fairly recent full citizenship-granted African American – to mention the possibility of childhood trauma can easily be met with contempt, ridicule and a defensive comparison of one's struggle against that of another. *"You think you have trauma? Well, until you've experienced XYZ, don't even talk to me about trauma!"*

Fortunately today, discussions about the scientific reality of mental health challenges connected to trauma are becoming more and more common throughout the country, allowing for more understanding on these subjects and less confusion, denial or shame. As of September 2017, the Substance Abuse and Mental Health Services Administration explains trauma as resulting from "an event, series of events, or set of circumstances that is experienced by an individual as physically or emotionally harmful or life threatening and that has lasting adverse effects on the individual's functioning and mental, physical, social, emotional, or spiritual well-being."
(https://www.samhsa.gov/trauma-violence)

Another author writes, "[A] trauma is any event or experience of sufficient force or magnitude that it overwhelms the capacity of the individual to absorb the experience and continue essentially unaffected, and which therefore results in a significant reduction or distortion of the individual's ability to carry on with NORMAL behavior, and to function adequately in their lives." (*Complex*

- 40 -

Trauma and Its Effects: Perspectives on Creating an Environment for Recovery, Robin Johnson (2012), Pavilion Publishing (Brighton) Ltd.)

Notice in this latter explanation that trauma affects the ability of an individual to "carry on with *normal* behavior." But what do we say when dysfunctional behavior is what is *normal* within a particular community? A person within that community who then experiences trauma ironically continues to carry on with their *normalized* maladaptive behavior. That abnormal behavior, which in another community would probably be identified as a response to trauma, can easily go undetected because, within this community, it is viewed as normal cultural behavior.

An example of this dynamic may be a person who chooses to continually self-medicate, staying intoxicated consistently throughout the day, just to ease the anxiety they may feel due to their living conditions and social environment. Since the majority of the inhabitants of that community make the same choice of staying *high* all day and night, and celebrate the joy and pleasure that comes from this choice, many may see this simply as a cultural norm, when in fact, for some it is an unhealthy, maladaptive coping mechanism to suppress the discomfort of the effects of trauma. This may help explain why so many of our young people today experience traumatic events as we did and are deeply affected, and yet they seem to carry on as they *normally* would on any other ordinary day. Their responses to trauma are camouflaged by the social norms of the greater community.

It seems psychological trauma can be more quickly defined than it can be identified. That's because currently there is no definitive measuring stick to declare what is universally a traumatic

41

experience and what is not. An event or experience that may be traumatic to one person may not have the same damaging effect on another. Since trauma is directly related to a person's stress level and their perception of their ability to cope, factors such as culture, past experiences, emotional support and paradigm can all play a role in whether they are in fact *traumatized* by an experience. Though trauma is scientifically supported, causes can still be very subjective.

The Crack Epidemic was a period in history that would change the world forever. Selfish ambition and violent behavior would become a common thread that plagued inner cities. Community division would leave neighborhoods fragmented and hostage to civil wars. And the effects of and response to trauma would become accepted as a cultural norm.

III. Trauma Organized Culture

I'm on the same corner where they pass dice,
same corner where they offer human sacrifice.
Same corner got us closer to the afterlife
and for a small fee you can rent a wife for half the
night. Right?
I pray to GOD I make my way through it,
The more you do wrong the easier it is to do it.

K-RAHN (MISSION)

Growing up, many of us belonged to families and homes that meant well but could not provide consistent safety, comfort and protection from the social ills of the communities in which we were being raised. Therefore, as children, and feeling vulnerable, we developed our own methods of coping that allowed us to survive and function day-to-day. In this feeling of vulnerability, we adapted our behavior and wore masks that made us feel safe. As kids, we didn't feel protected or supported by traditional moral authorities such as parents, pastors, law enforcement and school officials.

Instead, we felt alienated and often forced to conform to the value system of the streets before we ever had the opportunity to explore alternative identities. Due to extreme environmental and cultural factors, we often presented ourselves as one-dimensional, while many of our truer, unique, individual identities were never really allowed to develop.

However, though I grew up within street culture, I did not grow up in urban war zones. Apart from my short-term residence in South Central Los Angeles, every neighborhood I grew up in could be considered what I heard referred to in one of my college courses as "gilded ghettoes." These are neighborhoods that have the outward appearance of being decent, functional and supportive communities but inwardly contained much of the same dysfunctional, criminal and counter-productive characteristics you would expect to find in regions well known for blatant gang, drug and criminal activity. Gilded ghettoes are deceptive. These are working class communities that often border and blend with more impoverished and neglected communities.

In the 1980s and 1990s, the Crack Epidemic hit urban America like an atomic bomb, creating a similar social mushroom cloud effect as the actual weapon of mass destruction. Though its direct target was the southern region of Los Angeles, its devastation rapidly expanded with a vicious ripple effect, spreading outside its immediate boundaries into communities across the country.

Complex Trauma: From Neighborhoods To 'Hoods

With the presence of crack cocaine came a drastic change in the very character of previously thriving communities. Over time, people stopped being neighbors to one another, and neighborhoods became simply "'hoods." For those living in communities directly impacted by the Crack Epidemic, we saw the following characteristics often develop:

1. *The young teenager turned crack dealer* became more influential, arrogant, disrespectful, cold-hearted, greedy, violent, ruthless and powerful.

2. *The adult resident turned crack addict* became manipulative, cunning, desperate, child-like, an outcast, powerless, disrespected, dishonorable, unimportant and disinterested with the daily responsibilities for maintaining quality of life.

3. *The crack addict's child* felt abandoned, embarrassed, angry, traumatized, betrayed, confused and unappreciated.

4. *The uninvolved resident of a crack-impacted neighborhood* felt fearful, powerless to change the community,

voiceless, angry, unprotected, untrusting, hardened and confused.

5. *The crack dealer's friend* felt admiration, pride, and sometimes envy for the success of the crack dealer.

6. *The crack dealer's child* felt abandoned, loved, shame, pride, and confusion.

These awful, but somewhat common, characteristics surfaced throughout urban "'hoods" across America. Crack cocaine was not the first drug to damage the moral fiber of Black and Brown communities, and these characteristics were not new to urban settings. However, their rapid and widespread expansion and the corresponding destruction of community bonds across the nation, was new. So much unaddressed pain, shame, confusion and division resulted, which in turn brought about a sinister shift in paradigms and values. Survival, self-preservation and disregard for the wellbeing of others became a blatant focus of behavior.

Consequently, it became common for urban community residents to endure traumatic experiences in all of its multiple forms. The experiences of young people in particular intensified, possibly resulting into what is known as "complex trauma." According to the National Child Traumatic Stress Network, "The term *complex trauma* describes the problem of children's exposure to multiple or prolonged traumatic events and the impact of this exposure on their development." *(http://www.nctsn.org/trauma-*

types#q2) In such cases, the harm occurs by a caregiver or in the context of an interpersonal relationship.

Complex trauma is similar to the widely-known Post-Traumatic Stress Disorder (PTSD), most commonly diagnosed in military veterans, for example, when a soldier in battle engages in or witnesses disturbing war-time activities, such as violent death or torture, in a foreign land. This soldier may be so deeply affected by the incident that it hinders their ability to process what happened in a healthy way. This inability may lead to alarming reactions, such as flashbacks (mentally reliving the traumatic experience over and over again); avoidance of thoughts, places or objects that remind the person of the traumatic event; being easily startled; constantly feeling on edge; regular nightmares and angry outbursts; among other challenges. PTSD is a very serious disorder that can severely strain relationships and lead to the sufferer feeling extremely alienated or worse. (https://www.nimh.nih.gov/health/topics/post-traumatic-stress-disorder-ptsd/index.shtml)

As horrific as PTSD is, we must here acknowledge that for decades, young residents, including myself and my peer group, have been indirectly forced to grow up in communities where traumatic experiences are often considered *normal*. Furthermore, it's important to note that, unfortunately, unlike the traumatized war vet, some of these young people never leave the battlefield. Their urban war zone is not in a foreign land, thousands of miles away. Their war zone is not a place they get deployed to for a temporary tour of duty. For these kids, the war zone encompasses a place they call *home*. And *home* is a place where many of them are taught to strive to one day make it

47

out of before it kills them. For these young residents, the response is not *post*-traumatic, because they continue to experience traumatic events day after day.

I can recall a night during my teenage years when I and two of my friends were walking from my home to my friend's home. He lived only one block away from me. During this short walk, one my friends recognized the driver of a passing car and raised his hands in the air to greet him and say, "What's up." The car kept going. Within moments, a guy appeared from a distance and was walking towards us. We saw him but thought nothing of it. As we approached my friend's house, the guy was now within a few feet of us. With no warning he began shooting in our direction. Instinctively, we ran to take cover. The two friends I was with ran towards my friend's house, while I ran in the opposite direction towards my house. As I was running, I heard my friend yell, "It's me! Wait it's me!" Followed by more shots fired.

I ran up the block to my house and went into my room to grab my gun. As I shuffled through my hiding spot, my mother came in my room and asked me what I was doing. I told her I was looking for something and had to step back out to give it to my friend. As she left my room, I grabbed my pistol and stuffed it in my jacket pocket. I ran out the front door towards the area I'd just left, looking to check on my friend. As I got closer, I noticed police were already on the scene. I then turned around and immediately headed back home, trying not to move too quickly and draw attention to myself.

The next day I found out that my friend, whose voice I heard yell out, had been shot multiple times and was in the hospital in stable condition. Ironically, allegedly the shooter was a very close friend of his but was under the influence of drugs and did not recognize him. The guy was out "set tripping" and looking for someone to attack in honor of the gang he was a part of. Of course, when asked by police if any of us knew the shooter or if we were able to describe the shooter, we knew nothing.

I'm not sure if I can say I was traumatized by this incident or not. However, stories such as this are not rare. The kid who experiences running for his life while being shot at near a local bus stop, and sees his friend get shot multiple times during the mayhem, must walk past that same bus stop daily. He sees his friend's dried blood stain on the sidewalk for weeks until it eventually fades away. As he approaches this bus stop during his daily routine, it's possible he feels the anxiety of the potential threat of this kind of incident happening again. He knows the shooter and will probably see him again as they coinhabit common areas and venues of the community. In my case, I continued to walk this same route daily to my friend's house and did in fact see the alleged shooter after the incident.

Clearly, it is natural to feel afraid during and after a traumatic or potentially traumatic situation. The presence of fear can trigger automatic or natural reactions in the human body to help us avoid or defend ourselves against danger. One of those reactions is the increased production of *cortisol*. Labeled as the "stress hormone," cortisol helps with the "fight-or-flight" response to danger, a natural reaction of the body to help protect us from harm. As stated in a *Psychology Today* article titled "Cortisol: Why 'The Stress Hormone' Is Public Enemy No. 1," "Once the alarm to release cortisol has sounded, your body becomes mobilized and ready for action— but there has to be a *physical* release of fight or flight. Otherwise, cortisol levels build up in the blood which *wreaks havoc on your mind and body."* *(https://www.psychologytoday.com/blog/the-athletes-way/201301/cortisol-why-the-stress-hormone-is-public-enemy-no-1)*

When living in an environment where residents constantly feel unsafe, the constant threat, and perceived threat, of danger can keep them on continual alert, which in turn can potentially produce a chemical imbalance within both the brain and the body. Neuroscientists have discovered that each hemisphere of the brain holds a small section of nervous tissue that is responsible for detecting danger, called the *amygdala*. The amygdala is what scans the environment for threats and is involved in the processing and expression of emotions, such as anger, fear and anxiety. The more of a threat the environment is, or is perceived to be, for a person, the more active the amygdala becomes. Living in a community where the fear of violence, betrayal and harassment are common can lead to a continuous sounding of this neurological alarm system.

This may explain why many of us grow up with a heightened sense of suspicion about other people's motives and why we bear the burden of having what some refer to as "trust issues." I know firsthand what it's like to be so suspicious of those around me that I actually look for reasons not to trust them. Maybe it's the way they look at me, or their body language, or the "vibe" they give. All I know is, there is something about them that "I ain't feeling." Everybody, except for a very select few, was "suspect." And I treated them accordingly. For some of my peers, everyone, without exception was suspect.

Furthermore, exposure to traumatic events can cause the amygdala to override the brain's pre-frontal cortex, causing it to be on hyper-alert. The pre-frontal cortex is responsible for rational thought and intellect, while the amygdala is where one's emotional memory is stored. This means, for example, that for someone who's been viciously attacked by a dog that broke loose from its chain, throughout the course of their life, the sound of a chain rattling may instantly trigger them to be on intense alert or defense as the brain perceives and the body prepares for another dog attack.

In heavily gang- and drug-impacted communities, the brain and body work no differently. Imagine how devastating it can be to witness the rapid social, financial, moral and physical deterioration of a loved one who's become addicted to drugs. Imagine that same drug addicted loved one buying drugs from one of your drug-selling loved ones. Imagine the pain of suddenly losing a loved one who was murdered by someone you know among your peers, or even by another loved one. Imagine knowing about the murder and not being able to say anything about it, because in your community that would be frowned upon as "snitching," which has its consequences. Then, since telling authorities or your peers is not an option, but you still want to do something about it, imagine taking matters into your own hands. Imagine you're now the one causing other people the same pain you once felt. Imagine the other people then going through the same process and cycle that you just went through.

Then imagine not trusting law enforcement because, although they are said to protect and serve you, you know first-hand that many of them instead have, and will continue to, violate, harass and brutalize you and your peers. Imagine now losing a close friend to long-term incarceration because police caught him with a small amount of an unlawful substance. Imagine considering that this same unlawful substance is coming into your neighborhood from out of the country. Imagine questioning how this unlawful substance is getting into your country so frequently, in such large amounts, and then making it into your neighborhood. Imagine considering that very few people ever get arrested for bringing huge amounts of this unlawful substance in, while so many people in your community continue to get arrested for possessing such small amounts of it once it's here.

Imagine your government declaring a "war on drugs," which leads to a tremendous increase in the incarceration rate of your fellow community residents whom the "war on drugs" is supposed to protect, but with no decrease in the presence of drugs in the community and no improvement in community safety. Imagine this same "war on drugs" that is supposed to be in place to protect you, ironically, instead feels like a war *on you* and people who look like you.

Imagine popular music being made about your painful reality, distributed for the entire world to sing along and dance to. Imagine you and the entire world chanting lyrics that celebrate the death and destruction of your community. Imagine experiencing all of this as a child.

Under all these circumstances, how would you view the world? How would you view yourself? How protected would you feel? What would be your philosophy regarding "trust"? In terms of complex trauma, what stressors do you imagine you would have? What sounds, events, objects and situations would trigger an alarming reaction out of you? What do you think your reaction would be? Do you think you would react to these triggers in a way that could easily be perceived as overreaction?

What does a community do with all of this unaddressed, unacknowledged trauma? We suppress it until we either explode onto others or implode into ourselves.

Examples of Cultural Trauma Responses

Here are just some of the survival mantras that reflect the conditioning to anticipate the reoccurrence of pain and to proactively defend oneself against it:

> *"If somebody hits you, hit back harder."* – Why? If you let the assault go without consequence, then you'll continually be a victim.

> *"Never snitch."* – Why? Authority figures (teachers, administrators, law enforcement, etc.) do not have our best interests at heart and therefore should not be invited into matters that are between us. To invite them in is the ultimate betrayal.

> *"You can't trust anyone."* – Why? There is no honor amongst the community. Everyone is out for themselves and will betray you when it is to their benefit.

> *"Bomb first."* – Why? When you *sense* a confrontation arising, it is always best to attack them before they attack you.

> *"F- the police."* – Why? The history of brutality and unfair treatment by law enforcement against our community has resulted in an adversarial relationship between law enforcement and us.

Many urban community residents are taught these mantras well before we have an actual corresponding experience. However, with all this trauma and pain short-circuiting the relationships in our neighborhoods, it is important to take an honest look at the genocidal cycle perpetuating that trauma and pain, and what is being created as a result of it. Our pain may explain our dysfunction, but it does not fully justify it. Collectively, it must be declared that the destructive cultural norms and behavior in our community are unacceptable. Victimhood does not make one righteous by default.

The term *complex trauma* addresses how children's exposure to multiple or prolonged traumatic events impacts their ongoing development. It is important to emphasize that in complex trauma, the traumatic stressors are generally interpersonal, which means they are caused by other people with whom the victim has a relationship. To be deliberately violated by a person you know and even trust can be devastating. This is further true when you must continue to have some sort of relationship with the perpetrator during and well after the violation, and that person shows no sign of remorse or retribution. Such is often the case in communities where violence is commonly inflicted amongst neighboring and distantly neighboring residents, who know each other and may have had relationships with one another for years. Sadly, complex traumatic experiences have become so common that many communities have been pressured to accept them as a normal way of life.

Trauma-Organized Culture

Culture is the accumulation of behavioral patterns, arts, beliefs, institutions, language, trends, social expectations and all other fruits of human thought, philosophy and interaction. It is the sum character of a community's identity. It is by way of a population's *culture* that the wisdom and skills necessary for the survival of the community and its individual residents are shared. Consequently, culture can mold how we identify and interpret the threat of traumatic events and how we act out our responses to these events. (The National Association of School Psychologists, Cultural Perspectives on Trauma and Critical Response, adapted by Kris Sieckert, NCSP, NEAT Central Region Facilitator; http://www.nasponline.org/resources/crisis_safety/nea t_cultural.aspx)

For example, in one culture, it may be extremely traumatic to have someone pull out a gun and aim it at you, and it may be perfectly acceptable to outwardly express fear in the face of such a threatening situation. In another culture, such an experience may be more common and anticipated and therefore may be less traumatic at the time, but any display of fear may be considered inappropriate behavior and serve as justification to further prey upon and terrorize you.

When looking at some of the common, seemingly destructive teachings, values and social norms in heavily gang- and drug-impacted communities, we find that many of those norms are in place in response to certain traumas that are common in those communities. When we look even closer, we find a culture of pain and abuse but also of creativity, resilience, and survival.

55

Those seeking to serve these communities effectively must acknowledge and understand that they are serving communities that have endured a long history of various traumatic events over many generations. This consistent community trauma, endured by generation after generation, coupled with the normalization and expectation of re-occurring traumatic events, has led to the development of a *trauma-organized culture.* This is a culture that consciously and subconsciously creates social norms and values in response to the common traumas and toxic stress of their community. As Dr. Sandra L. Bloom references in her book, *Creating Sanctuary in the School,* (1995) quoting the work of Dr. Arnon Bentovim:

> "As we learned more about the profoundly negative impact of traumatic experience on generation after generation within a family, we realized that many of our social systems, including the family, are "trauma organized" (Bentovim, 1992). By this we mean that the repeated experience of trauma becomes one of the central organizing experiences in the individual, in the family, and in larger social groups."

As we grow up in these environments, not only do we who share similar traumatic experiences tend to gravitate to each other, but also our thoughts, feelings, expectations, customs and paradigms become shaped by the anticipation of and defense against those common traumatic experiences and the toxic stress they generate. Our mental framework becomes rooted in the quest for survival. Our very character is morphed into the mold of the social climate of the 'hood, often disallowing certain characteristics that may not fit this mold to be left underdeveloped.

It's akin to what we observe in nature, where certain crops can only be brought forth in certain conditions and climates. For instance, we see oranges and other citrus fruits grow in tropical and subtropical climates, though they would not stand a chance of sustainable growth in freezing arctic climates. Carrots are a cool-weather vegetable that requires the right temperatures to produce a healthy crop. Same applies to human personality and social characteristics. In a climate of distrust, manip-ulation, exploitation, poverty and violence, how does society expect to grow a harvest of emotional balance, love, contentment, peace and productivity? As seen with vegetation, certain human qualities are more easily brought forth in certain [social] climates and conditions than in others.

Psychopathic: To Be Or Not To Be?

Working with teenagers and young adults has helped keep me current in my awareness on the latest cultural trends, music and fashion. I often engage in discussions with young people about rap music and who the hottest artists currently are. In these discussions, they eagerly point me to videos and songs posted online by their favorite rap artists. For many of these youngsters, the content of their favorite rap artists is the same as the content of my childhood favorites.

Topics and themes include:

- *how tough I am*
- *what violent act I'll commit against anyone who disrespects me*
- *what kind of gun I have*
- *who I'm going to rob*
- *who I'm going to kill*
- *what sexual acts I'll engage in with women*
- *the relegation of women as sexual objects*
- *why women don't deserve respect*
- *the idea that no one can be trusted*
- *how I'm going to be rich by any means necessary*
- *why it's important not to have feelings for anyone*
- *having no mercy on others is a virtue*
- *in life, you must con your way to the top*
- *I love my homeboys, but remember, even homies will betray you*
- *the legal system is against me*
- *the more drugs you sell, the more rich and powerful you become*
- *life is about money, power, sex and respect (towards me)*
- *I can smoke more weed (or consume more drugs) than anybody*
- *I stay high all the time*

- *life is all about my personal happiness, even at the expense of others*
- *love is a weakness*
- *you are to resort to extreme violence at the first sign of disrespect*
- *murder is no big deal.*

Reflecting on the fact that these have been the undisputed themes of many of the rap songs that I and my peers have listened to for over two decades, I started to question how healthy, or unhealthy, it is to normalize such ideologies in culture. Working with young people and listening to teen boys recite song after song about what kind of gun they have and who they were going to kill really made me think. Analyzing this normalization, coupled with my own personal experiences of living in America's gang- and drug-impacted urban culture, led me to consider the concept of antisocial personality disorder, or what many may refer to as *psychopathy* or *sociopathy*.

According to Steve Bressert, Ph.D., in an article published on PsychCentral.com titled *Antisocial Personality Disorder Symptoms*:

> Antisocial personality disorder (APD) is a disorder that is characterized by a long-standing pattern of disregard for other people's rights, often crossing the line and violating those rights. A person with antisocial personality disorder (APD) often feels little or no empathy toward other people and doesn't see the problem in bending or breaking

the law for their own needs or wants. The disorder usually begins in childhood or as a teen and continues into a person's adult life."
(https://psychcentral.com/disorders/a ntisocial-personality-disorder-symptoms/)

Pondering on symptoms related to APD, I began to consider that though there are individuals whose display of this disorder would qualify them for a mental health diagnosis, there are many other people whose personality has become what could *resemble* APD simply due to the consistent influence of antisocial behavior and expectation in their surroundings, that of trauma-organized culture. Some of the most prevalent symptoms related to APD (psychopathy or sociopathy) that I read are:

- Disregard for society's laws
- Violation of the physical or emotional rights of others
- Lack of stability in job and home life
- Lack of remorse
- Superficial wit and charm
- Recklessness and impulsivity

In popular (pop) culture, both sociopathy and psychopathy are chiefly characterized by a severe deficiency or complete lack of conscience regarding other people. However, when looking at gang- and drug-impacted urban culture, particularly of the 1990s, I find that many of us were taught or conditioned to *consciously and purposely* work to develop many of the harmful and dangerous behavior patterns often associated with APD (sociopathy or psychopathy) in spite of conscience.

What is most interesting is that a hidden reality exists in the minds of many young people who outwardly embrace and display antisocial behaviors due to environment. Though their *behaviors* may point to psychopathy, many of these individuals in fact do *not* lack conscience at all but instead see their conscience as a *liability*.

For me and my peers, many of us felt as if we were forced to deny and suppress our conscience until it finally became easier to exercise antisocial behavior. Criminal activity and disregard for others usually doesn't come naturally. Some perpetrators start off by going against their own personal moral convictions until it gets easier and easier to do. They eventually become emotionally numb to the guilt. In our constant quest to achieve the royal status of being considered "real," people like me, who had a strong conscience that constantly spoke out and discouraged me from engaging in certain acts – or going "too far" with certain acts – would begin to internally second-guess our own authenticity. *Why do I care about the well-being of others when I'm taught I'm not supposed to? They don't care about me, so why do I care about them? Is this consideration for the wellbeing of others a sign of weakness?*

Though many of us did not grow up suffering from a psychopathic mental disorder, we did grow up in the hands of a culture that reinforced psychopathic behavior as a perceived means for survival and prosperity. Trauma can be a double-edged sword, because often the perpetrator as well as the victim is negatively affected, though in different ways and to different degrees. This is not to equalize the trauma between the perpetrator and the victim. However, I do make the important point that we inherited a trauma-organized paradigm that exalted antisocial personality as a cultural standard.

Though I grew up with a strong support system in my mother and managed to avoid being utterly destroyed by this culture, I did not escape being singed by its fiery, consuming blaze. It is very important to acknowledge that for youth in almost any culture, peer acceptance and high reputation often trumps all. Both youth and even some adults have a pressing need to answer the call of peer pressure. In these environments, social ranking not only determines status but often determines survival. It determines whether you have a healthy and safe daily social experience or a tormented one. The lower you are on the social totem pole, the less you get in life. Living by these de facto terms leaves a young person with little to no will to resist and overcome the conditions around him. And that's where groupthink comes in.

Groupthink

The word "groupthink" was coined in an article of the same name by William H. Whyte, Jr., in *Fortune* magazine back in March 1952. Much of the initial formal research on groupthink was conducted years later by Irving Janis, a research psychologist from Yale University. According to the online encyclopedia, Wikipedia, as of the writing of this book, groupthink is explained as:

> a psychological phenomenon that occurs within a group of people in which the desire for harmony or conformity in the group causes irrational or dysfunctional decision-making. Group members strive to

minimize discord and reach a consensus decision without critical evaluation of alternative viewpoints by actively, and even aggressively, suppressing opposing viewpoints, and by isolating themselves from outside influences. Groupthink requires individuals to avoid raising controversial issues or alternative solutions, and there is loss of individual creativity, uniqueness and independent thinking.
https://en.wikipedia.org/wiki/Groupth ink (March 8, 2017)

Keeping It Real

More than anything, my generation and peer group strived with all that we had in us to be deemed as "real" by both ourselves and our peers. More explicitly, we strived at all costs to earn the highly exalted and coveted label of "real nigga." Through daily conversation, coupled with the repetitious sounds of hypnotic rap songs infused with street doctrine that propagated the invulnerability of being real, many in our generation were willing to risk life, future stability and freedom to attain to this perceived honor. Groupthink taught us that striving for this status was a *moral obligation* that was worthy of any undesirable consequences that came with our actions. Death (in all of its forms) before dishonor.

Remember, for adolescents, the need for acceptance from peers is often a more powerful priority than personal safety or long-term achievement. So, those in the community who didn't live according this exalted code of living were often considered weak, uncool and outcasts. Those who spoke against it were considered "haters" or "soft." Consequently, as stated before, many youth don't have the will or communal support to resist the groupthink around them, so they assimilate.

In our pursuit of realness and to keep the cohesion of the group, many of my peers and I consciously or subconsciously chose to self-sabotage. Since "real niggas" are known to refuse to assimilate to mainstream White culture, we consciously and subconsciously rejected anything that resembled or felt like *selling out*. Real niggas stay true and loyal to their loved ones and to the code of the streets at all costs.

"Real niggas don't give a f---," we would say, because we didn't care about how the world viewed us, nor were we scared of the consequences of our actions. Real niggas openly rebelled against much of the values, trends and expectations of mainstream culture – including institutional education; trendy, widely acceptable fashion, so-called proper etiquette, mundane employment and even socially acceptable attitudes. Angry at feeling isolated, undervalued and abandoned, our culture was characterized by a consistent expression of rebellion.

Sadly, many of us refused to apply ourselves in school, not because it was too difficult but because we did not want to assimilate. We did not see ourselves in the curriculum in any way, nor did we see how school could help us achieve our particular ambitions, so we saw little to no value in getting a public education. We rebelled against what we saw as the "whitewashing" of our minds. We spoke loudly, with aggression and disrespect. We refused to wear our pants at a level that we considered too high above our waist. We dreamed of being mob bosses, drug kingpins, rappers, athletes and casino owners – ambitions that we thought did not require success in, or assimilation to, the traditional mainstream White culture.

Ironically, though individuals make up the community, it is often the community that dictates to the individual what his or her values and customs should be. I'm sure many people who aspire or have aspired to be a real nigga have considered that violence is causing more pain in our community than healing. I'm sure they've considered it highly inappropriate and degrading to continually identify oneself as a "nigga" or to refer to women with a whole list of damaging but commonly used terms. I'm sure it's been considered that much of what many in our communities lived and died for was not worth our life or imprisonment.

However, the culture around us has told us it was worth it ... and so did many of the most influential and well-funded spokespeople of the culture. Namely, rap stars, who to us were like real-life, mythical super heroes. In addition, our favorite characters in our favorite urban films were blasted across the silver screen, larger than life, indirectly but surely reinforcing the same message. This is not to say that our mindset was the fault of any individual. It instead reveals that many people played either a direct or indirect, intentional or unintentional role in perpetuating this groupthink. Art imitates life and life imitates art.

Confining ourselves to the boundaries and expectations of the consuming culture around us, many of us carried within our being severe self-limiting beliefs, which led to a vicious cycle of self-doubt, lack of purpose, lack of motivation and more self-sabotaging. Interestingly, however, the common bond of victimhood and oppression and the

65

demeaning self-image we all seemed to share strangely kept us somewhat unified, although in an extremely dysfunctional way. We were all lost, trying to find our path. We were all abandoned in some sense of the word. We all felt antagonized by mainstream white culture. We all felt the odds were stacked against us.

College Bound

I don't take for granted the fact that having a mother who was committed to my success played a major role in the development of the man I am today. Since I was a young child, she would repeatedly speak to me about me going to college and one day becoming an entrepreneur. She would constantly tell me, "You don't go to school and get an education, so you can work for someone else," and then affirm, "A winner never quits and a quitter never wins." I heard these words almost daily. So, though I was psychologically entangled in the groupthink of the immediate culture around me, at home I was being fed a positive self-image that countered many limiting and counter-productive messages of my community. Also, from preschool through the age of six I was also enrolled in Omowale Ujamaa Shule, an African centered school that taught the value of Black history and strong character. Though this was for a short period in my educational life, it laid a strong and solid foundation that would forever be with me.

I always knew I would go to college. How I would get there was the question. I remember in my junior year of high school my mom telling me to go talk to my academic counselor about the requirements for college enrollment. I honored her request and scheduled an appointment. The counselor was an older African American woman with a short, natural hairstyle and a no-nonsense personality. She reminded me of the socially conscious women that I used to see at the African centered school I attended as a young child. At first glance, I thought to myself she was the perfect person to talk to and would understand my struggle and guide me in the way I needed.

When we met, I remember us sitting down across from each other at her desk as she reviewed my transcripts. I'm sure I was reeking with the smell of marijuana and probably had red, bloodshot eyes. She said very little to me during our greeting. With her head down, she scrolled through the document while making statements like, "I see you have a D here and another here. You didn't do well in this class. Hmm." When she finally raised her head, she looked at me as said, "You can't go to college with grades like this." Then she stared at me. I replied, "So what should I do?" She responded, "I don't know. Maybe you can *try* to enroll in a community college or something." I simply said, "Okay" and ended our meeting. I left her office feeling defeated, thinking, *Man, now what?*

That evening, I shared with my mom what happened in the meeting. I remember her getting upset and instructing me to talk to another counselor. So, I did. A week or two later I met with the college counselor, Mrs. Ramsey, an older white woman who at the time looked very mean to me. She looked much older than the academic counselor I previously spoke with. As I stepped into her office, with my jeans heavily starched and creased, T-shirt crisp, and the white walls of my Chuck Taylors and circle laces clean, I assumed this meeting would be a waste of time. I was only going through with it to make my mom happy. I didn't want to meet. It was during lunch period and this was the time I made most of my money during the school day. I had stuff to sell and a staircase dice game to join.

We sat down at Mrs. Ramsey's desk, and again, I'm sure I was reeking with the strong scent of marijuana. "Hi, young man. How are you?" she greeted me. Through my ruby tinted eyes, I looked at her and replied, "Fine." She pulled out my transcripts and said, "Let's take a look at what we have here." I sat there quietly as she reviewed my file. As she scanned the document, she didn't say anything to me. If I remember correctly, she simply hummed a song to herself. Then she looked at me and said, "Well, kiddo, what college are you interested in attending?" I didn't know. It really didn't matter to me. So, I said the first ones that came to mind. "Uh...UCLA, USC or Notre Dame." She said "Ok. Let's look at the requirements for those schools."

As Mrs. Ramsey and I went one by one looking at the requirements, it was clear to me that I was not academically fit to get accepted into any of these schools. She then asked me, "Have you considered applying for a state school?" I had no idea what that meant. "What's that?" I asked. She explained to me that the schools I listed were private universities while state schools were public universities and weren't as strict with their enrollment process. "Let's look at some of the requirements for state universities in California." We looked at schools in San Jose, Sacramento, Los Angeles, Long Beach and San Diego.

She then pointed out the grade point average requirement of these schools and explained to me that the lower my grade point average is, the higher I must score on a test called the SAT, Scholastic Assessment Test. Then she said, "Based on your current transcripts, you're ineligible to attend any of these schools, but if you want to attend, here's what you must do." She walked me through my transcript and pointed out each class that needed to be made up through either summer school or Saturday school. She told me I could enroll in extra elective courses such as the Regional Occupation Program to get easy A's to help boost up my grade point average. She then went to explain that for these schools, if your grade point average is "x," then the score you need on your SAT to qualify would be "y." Though this woman looked mean to me in the beginning, ironically, I noticed that the more she talked, the nicer she looked.

I left Mrs. Ramsey's office with a burst of energy, hope and confidence that I'd never felt before regarding my education. I was now committed to a purpose! I knew what I had to do. The blueprint was laid out for me and it was up to me whether or not I'd put in the work necessary to make it happen. I now had a clear, tangible and attainable *why* for applying myself in my school work.

It is so important that those seeking to help young people approach them with a nonjudgmental and optimistic attitude. Those contrasting experiences with the two counselors made it evident that ethnicity and age are not necessarily determining factors in the success of youth engagement. Instead, I found that sincere care for young people and not only belief in their potential but the ability to identify their potential to them are what often make youth engagement effective. As adults and professionals, we have to find the potential in young people's lives and help them see it, believe it and pursue it.

Though my behavior and work ethic regarding school improved only slightly after those meetings with my counselors, I completed the courses needed to improve my transcripts. I followed Mrs. Ramsey's advice, enrolling in Saturday school, retaking a 9th grade English class, and summer school to complete a Geometry requirement. I also enrolled in both a seventh period drama class and the after school Regional Occupational Program to help boost my grade point average. I would check in with Mrs. Ramsey periodically to update her on my progress. With the pressing reinforcement of my mother, I also reluctantly took the SAT, though I was extremely intoxicated from the late night I had before. Somehow, I did well on it. Thank God.

Now, with a decent SAT score coupled with an improved grade point average, I met my goal and was qualified to be accepted in a California State University! I applied to a few state campuses and was accepted and actually even had the option to choose which college I would attend. I chose San Diego State University.

According to the Substance Abuse and Mental Health Services Administration (SAMHSA), the agency within the U.S. Department of Health and Human Services that leads public health efforts to advance the behavioral health of the nation, the six principles that the trauma informed approach is built on are *(1) Safety, (2) Trustworthiness, (3) Peer support (4) Collaboration, (5) Empowerment/ Choice and (6) Cultural, historical and gender Issues*. Reflecting on my interactions with Mrs. Ramsey I must say that she intuitively put these principles to practice. From our introduction, up until my high school graduation, she continuously helped me to feel safe meeting with her. I never felt judged or belittled. Her gentle honesty in explaining to me that at the time I was ineligible to be accepted to a university proved her to be trustworthy. Her support in researching the requirements of each college I desired to go, regardless of how far I was from qualifying, and explaining what I needed to do to become eligible was key in offering me hope. Encouraging me to check in and update her on my progress, as she cheered me on and guided me throughout the process was such an important collaboration that sent my confidence through the roof. Letting me know that though I was currently ineligible to be accepted to a university, there were steps I could take to make me eligible empowered me and offered me the choice to either do what it takes to achieve this goal, or not. Lastly, not once did I feel she stereotyped me or disregarded me for aligning with the cultural norms of my community.

I doubt that Mrs. Ramsey was formally educated in what is now called trauma informed care. If she was not, she is truly a testament that in this regard, the science of today is finally catching up to the practices of the those who have been effective in youth engagement for decades. Her approach came from a place of love and care. And I'm sure that it is people like her from which the trauma informed framework is based on.

True character change for me came about during my college years. For me, the detrimental effects of groupthink were slowly overcome as a result of being removed for a time, from communities where this particular way of thinking reigned. Ironically, during my initial arrival in San Diego, though there for education, I found myself congregating with the same type of individuals who ascribed to the groupthink I was accustomed to. I connected with the "realest niggas" I could find.

71

Some attended the university, but most of them did not go to school at all. Most were street guys from other cities in California who were now in San Diego because their girlfriends were going to school and they saw living with her as an opportunity to get away from the 'hood and lay low for a minute. They saw the college area as fertile ground for many different hustles. Others were street guys I crossed paths with who lived in the city. As the saying goes, "Birds of a feather flock together."

Though this was the company I kept, being placed in an environment that encouraged growth and critical thinking in particular was great for me. People often silence themselves in group discussion about cultural norms because they think their reputations will suffer or they'll be penalized for not going along with the way things have always been. Now being somewhat out of my previous environment, I was afforded the privilege to self-reflect and analyze life in a way I had never done before. Establishing a critical thinking culture is essential to breaking the boundaries of groupthink.

As time went on, I began to read and isolate myself from others more and more, and in the process, I began to discover my own self-worth and develop cultural pride and a strong sense of responsibility to better my community. I began reading books about African history, Black American history, spirituality, religion, conspiracy theories and philosophy. I watched documentaries and listened to debates and interviews. I was becoming somewhat of a young intellectual. In the presence of this new found inner light, the invisible ropes of the groupthink that once bonded me so tightly to street culture were slowly melting away like wax in the presence of fierce heat. By choice, I became an outsider to the only culture I knew as my own.

IV. It Ain't Nothin Like Hip Hop Music

I built this country still I'm treated as half a man
Rather be called 'nigga' than be called an African.
Laughin when a joke is made about my own kind
I have to win, but secondary in my own mind.

K-RAHN (WHY)

As I stated, Hip Hop music and Hip-Hop culture have had an extreme influence on my life, environment, paradigm and peer group. The same holds true for younger generations. With less parental influence and less respect towards school teachers and civic workers, today's entertainers, specifically rappers, have much of our youth's attention. They therefore have become our youth's teachers and leaders by default, whether they want to be or not . . . and whether we choose to acknowledge it or not.

I'm not saying it's a rapper's responsibility to be a leader or teacher. I'm saying that due to his or her influence, he or she *is* a leader or teacher by default. In a perfect world, all children's parents would teach their children angelic values to counteract any destructive values that are introduced and reinforced in entertainment. But we do not live in a perfect world, and anybody who works with heavily gang- and drug-impacted communities knows that many of our kids are raised with values that are far from angelic.

In today's society, the Black male rapper is often perceived by youth as the freest and coolest man in the world. He smokes as he pleases, drinks what he pleases, buys what he pleases, disrespects whomever he pleases, has as much sex as he pleases with whomever he pleases, freely engages in criminal activities, has the fanfare of all ethnicities around the world, sets global pop culture trends, lives a life of luxury, gets paid lots of money to have fun, creates and performs music, and is still unapologetically a *nigga*. Rappers are perceived to be free to be themselves in their rawest, and sometimes lowest, form and still succeed. It's no mystery why they have the admiration of the masses.

Niggaz 4 Life

Before I continue, I feel it's necessary to address the term *nigga,* which is so pervasive in rap music. As we know, the term is a variation of the degrading and even oppressive term *nigger*, which has been widely used and embraced for centuries by racist members of the white European, American and other populations for centuries. This word "nigger" has been used to describe, define and declare a degrading status for Black African people who were kidnapped and forcibly brought to the Americas. It is a term used to declare the perceived legal, social, intellectual and even biological inferiority of Black people all over the world.

For years, many people who use the term "nigga" have tried to argue that there is a difference between "nigger" and "nigga," and that simply changing the suffix of the word from "-er" to "-a" is enough to totally change the definition and context. I myself grew up in this culture in which the use of "nigga" has been justified and embraced, so I understand the explanation, though I do not fully agree with it. I find that though the explanation does have some validity, we as Black people have not been fully truthful in our acceptance of it.

In this discussion, it must be noted that Black people in this country were stripped of our identity as Africans while for centuries also being denied the right to identify as Americans. For centuries, we were then forced to answer to and identify with the term *nigger*. This term is, unfortunately, one of the only consistent titles for identification we've had since the American slave trade. Therefore, after being so deeply embedded into our psyche, it comes as no surprise that over time we began to accept this label as part of our own identity. Not wanting to fully embrace the degradation attached to this identity, but not yet ready to cast it off after we've been defined by it for the last 400 or so years, we have attempted to reshape, redefine and remix the term to better suit our liking. So we use a variation of it: *nigga*. It is still degrading and still implies inferiority, but with less of a sting.

Ironically, both *nigger* and *nigga* acknowledge a certain type of second-class citizenship, though one more blatantly than the other. Both terms acknowledge that racism and classism have relegated Black people to somewhat of a second-class status.

However, the difference between identifying oneself as a nigga versus a nigger is found mainly in the opposing attitudes that these two terms suggest. I'll explain this shortly. A person will claim that the word *nigga* is positive, then turn around and say something like, "No matter how much money you get, you're still a *nigga*." Clearly, there is no positive meaning in the latter statement. Likewise, some readily embrace "nigga" as a term of endearment amongst their fellow community members but then will be totally offended if someone outside their ethnicity or culture refers to them by this same term. This shows that such people have accepted the title or identity of being a nigga but also know that it still represents a degraded status in society.

So, if both variations of the term acknowledge second-class citizenship, why is the "-er" more offensive than the "-a?" It's because of the less than noble characteristics associated with the "-er" versus the somewhat noble characteristics that have come to be associated with the "-a." Again, it is the difference in attitudes.

The following chart illustrates some of these contrasting characteristics:

The "N-Word"	
Nigger	**[Real] Nigga**
Docile	Aggressive
Disloyal	Loyal to one's own
Submissive	Rebellious
Bottom class	Less than 1st class
Ignorant/Naïve	Street smart, Witty/Clever
Powerless	Powerful amongst the underclass
Worthless	Sense of worth, Trend setter
Accepts poverty	Hustles, Ambitious
Victim/Prey	Predator, Resilient
Fearful/Cowardly	Brave/Fearless

This contrast can be seen in the name of the group, N.W.A., or Niggas With Attitude. They're saying, "Yeah, we accept and acknowledge that we're *niggas*, but we have attitude and won't just lie down and be victimized. We're redefining what the word means." As with so many facets of life, the usage of the word is yet another instance where Black people in America have endured dire circumstances and have attempted to make the best of it. It reminds me of stories I've heard about pigs being cleaned and cut in preparation for the meals of slave masters, while the undesirable parts of the pig's body – the ears, the feet and the intestines – were discarded with the garbage. Those enslaved, in desperate need to eat, would find these discarded body parts, such as the intestines, and prepare them for their own meals (e.g., chitterlings). Now, ironically, we find that after generations of this practice, to some these same body parts have become a delightful treat, a delicacy. However, regardless of how well they are cleaned and seasoned, or how good they may taste to some, they are still pig intestines.

Urban Alchemy: What Makes Hip Hop So Special?

Now back to Hip Hop. For many of my peers and me, rappers were our heroes. Remember, many of the artists who reached Hip Hop stardom were teenagers and young adults themselves, who grew up in the same environments as we did, experienced the same trauma as we did if not worse, and were taught to uphold the same values, codes and customs as we were. They were now the voice to help further reinforce the paradigm.

Hip Hop as a culture extends far beyond music, though music is the medium through which the doctrine and value system are most commonly shared. In light of the fact that "culture" relates to common beliefs, customs, arts and entertainment, fashion, language, styles, perspectives, activities, etc., there is much debate about what defines "Hip Hop Culture" in particular. Some Hip Hop purists point to the original four activities, or elements, Hip Hop was founded on: emceeing, dj-ing, breakdancing and graffiti. Other purists also include the founding principles of peace, love, unity and having fun. When considering these founding elements and principles, many people are left to question whether or not much of the current mainstream rap music is truly *Hip Hop*. For myself, I acknowledge the concepts of evolution (and even mutation) and recognize that nothing remains the same, and I therefore choose not to enter such debates. Nonetheless, the founding concept that I recognize in Hip Hop beyond all others is this: "Making something out of nothing!"

To much of the world, this is the magic of Hip Hop. It is the alchemical ability to make something out of nothing that has mesmerized this nation and the world. The nation was amazed at how Hip-Hop pioneers used their parents' old funk records to find short snippets of songs and then "sample" them and mix them together with other snippets of songs to make full length instrumentals. The nation was intrigued by graffiti artists who used spray paint to create art on the sides of subway trains and cleverly turned them into moving canvases which toured their artwork all throughout their cities. The nation was fascinated with how kids would turn an ordinary sidewalk into a dancefloor and express themselves through a seemingly mystical style of performing art called "breakdancing." The nation, and soon the world, was stunned at how poor and often formally uneducated kids could formulate and manipulate words to their will, to tell vivid stories of pain and pleasure, while simultaneously maintaining consistent, alluring tones, rhythmic flows and rhyming patterns.

It is also important to mention here that rebellion against mainstream culture has also been a very concrete principle of early Hip Hop culture. It's ironic that a culture founded on rebelling against the mainstream culture is now dominating the mainstream and pop culture with tales of materialism, success and excessive luxury. However, to an extent, even this is a form of rebellion. The excess materialism and flaunting in much of modern Hip Hop is a form of rebellion because it comes from a people who historically are presumably not supposed to have it. Even though material success can be very illusory, the world questions, "How can a rapper with little formal education start off poor and hustling drugs on a street corner in his housing projects, end up using his talents and wit to position himself as a hustler in a corner office in the corporate world?"

This is magical! Throughout the years, Hip Hop fans and critics alike have witnessed this culture grow from humble beginnings as a local art form for poor Black and Brown kids in impoverished neighborhoods, to a global cultural cash cow that is embraced by every ethnicity of every tax bracket on every populated continent. The songs of poverty, struggle and pain of previous years turned into songs of wealth, success and victory. America is the global capital for people who seek to make something out of nothing, and Hip Hop became the soundtrack!

Gangsta Rap: As American As Apple Pie

Though I sometimes speak about how much of mainstream Hip Hop was hi-jacked and has tainted the images of manhood and success specifically to African American youth, it is important that I highlight that I do not blame any form of Hip Hop as the root of any problems in America. I must also point out that Hip Hop music itself has never been one-dimensional, though it's often promoted that way. I do not place moral judgment on Hip Hop, nor do I defend it or condemn it. It is what it is and will be what it will be.

When addressing our youth and Hip-Hop culture, it is essential to shift from thinking that rappers are always speaking *to* the youth to considering that sometimes rappers are speaking *for* the youth. Though as I stated, many rappers are looked to as leaders, the rapper is not always the one convincing a generation of what ambitions and values they should have. There are plenty other factors in society, such as the system of capitalism, that do this. Instead, many artists are actually reflecting ambitions and values that many of our young people already hold, which is why the young people, and old, gravitate to it. As stated before, many rappers actually come from the same groupthink and environments as the kids and adults they are now speaking to. Yes, the music does help perpetuate and solidify these values, but very rarely if ever does it create them.

People are drawn to music that connects with our values. We're attracted to what we agree with and are repelled by what we disagree with. However, many of the vulgar themes we hear and secretly like in Hip Hop are often themes that some of us would rather not admit to connecting with. I'm sure there

83

are certain ideals, lifestyles and values that many listeners are totally against and if songs promoted these ideals, those people would not support them regardless of how great the beat is.

In particular, it's interesting that many people connect with songs that overtly and nonchalantly discuss killing Black men and degrading Black women. Unfortunately, such treatment towards Black men and women has been perpetually accepted, practiced and celebrated since the inception of America. Black death and degradation have been a form of American entertainment for centuries. Throughout the years I've heard multiple Black rappers be so frank as to pridefully compare themselves to a Ku Klux Klanman or Nazi because of how much they either hate or kill niggas. So, the question becomes, "Does the message of Black death subconsciously connect with the values of the listeners?" If one was to replace the word "nigga" in a Hip-Hop song with a degrading word about another ethnicity, the context of the song would immediately change, and the masses would most likely be highly offended.

It seems there are two things critics of rap music are most upset about: Number one is the popularity of certain rap songs. Or, more specifically, of certain rap artists who make certain songs. People may not be as mad at the content of the songs as they are at the attention and influence rappers get from making songs with certain content. If a rapper makes a song about something some people consider offensive or foolish, no one cares until hundreds of thousands of people start supporting it. Then the critic goes after the rapper and bashes him or her for their wackness or the foolishness of their content. However, the question is, why did so many thousands of people in our society gravitate to this song? Even further, why was so much effort and money invested by corporations to ensure the popularity of the song? The artists, the corporate machine and the fans all have roles in what is accepted and trendy in today's music scene.

The second problem many people have with mainstream rap is often not the values rap artists promote, but the *way* they promote them. The overt and unapologetic honesty in rap is what many critics find offensive. What's interesting about this is the apparent contradiction. In looking at the history and social context of a society that was built on forced chattel slave labor, colonialism, misogyny, kidnapping, violence, theft and war, we find that greater America is fundamentally not offended by a value system that thrives on greed, violence, self-indulgence, the exploitation of others, profiting on the oppression of fellow human beings, womanizing or crime. And yet, it just seems to not want the masses to blatantly promote these values or declare them acceptable. In other words, our society outwardly protests such values while inwardly promoting them.

How do you think such confusion and contradiction in the landscape of morality affect our youth?

I've always loved so-called "gangsta rap." As I mentioned, I grew up on it. But as I've gotten older and more mature and analytical in my thinking, I have begun to question gangsta rap's effect on the community it supposedly represents. I ponder, how does it affect a people's psyche, self-esteem and self-image when the causes and triggers of their present-day trauma are packaged as material to entertain the world? How does it affect a people's psyche when the whole world is dancing to their pain and destruction?

85

As much as I have enjoyed the music, I must acknowledge that the corporation-funded gang and drug culture, being firmly embedded in the music, has kept the drug dealer's voice constantly in our ears. His perspective and teachings became our doctrine. He understood us, and we understood him. He felt our pain, and we felt his. And so it is also with the killer, the pimp, the player and the gangsta. Through music, he offered insights on matters of life when our fathers and uncles didn't. He became the "big homie" and even the father figure. Now, his influence has extended beyond the ear of the kid on the block and has traveled into the households of kids throughout the world.

However, we must be clear: much of Hip Hop culture is simply an exaggerated expression of American culture, rooted firmly in early American values. If you take an honest look at American history, you will see that the addiction to violence, materialism and power is an American thought process. Los Angeles rapper Nipsey Hussle sums it up perfectly when he says in a song titled *Keys to the City,* "bein' broke is so un-American!"

Likewise, misogyny and the disrespect towards women have been a part of American entertainment for a very long time. Think of the infamous Looney Tunes cartoon character, Pepe Le Pew, who vigorously chased after a voiceless *cat,* only to catch her and force himself on her, aggressively kissing and squeezing her as she desperately, but still silently, fought him off. Strangely, he was depicted as a romantic. What imagery to embed in a young child in his or her development. That same sort of "manifest destiny" ideology of the early American settlers – that I am destined by God to expand and conquer by any means necessary – is very present in Hip Hop culture.

Throughout history, many immigrants came to America with their own set of values, native to their homeland, that have since been passed down from generation to generation. In contrast, enslaved Africans in America, stripped of native values and culture, were not able to pass down homeland customs to the same degree or with the same degree of freedom. So then, the question now becomes, *From where did most Black people inherit and develop its modern culture?*

The answer: From our unique American experience. Over time, we had to rewire our whole value system based on the unique circumstances of our existence here in America, with very little wisdom that extend beyond American shorelines. So, we find that the Hip Hop culture started with the youth of urban Black and Brown America expressing their American experiences, values and aspirations through dance, visual art and Rhythm and Poetry (R.A.P.). In short, hate it or love it, rap music is as true to the American experience as it gets!

I Do What I Feel And I Do What I Like

Though the rapper is often portrayed as being free of all accountability to society and the consequences of his actions, I question how the pursuit of such freedoms in real life affects our youth. I used to always wonder why my generation and generations after us weren't as politically and intellectually *seasoned* as those during the Civil Rights Era.

I've concluded that, for one, many of us didn't feel the immediate threat of blatant racism as our previous generations did, which left us somewhat deluded about our progress and status in society. For two, coupled with the devastating effects of the crack epidemic, in recent days, youth are often so flooded by distractions from open access to drugs, guns, pornography, sex, violence and entertainment that many don't find the opportunity to think clearly. Kids today literary have computers in their pockets and immediate access to any virtual vice their hearts desire.

It reminds me of Disney's version of the Pinocchio story. In the movie, Pinocchio was led by his friend to a place called Pleasure Island. On Pleasure Island, Pinocchio and several other kids around his age were given the freedom by the Island landlord to smoke cigars, drink alcohol and play pool. It was a lawless land that seemed to offer no consequence for reckless activity.

As he and his peers enjoyed the intoxicating pleasures the island provided, Pinocchio began to notice that he and his friend were slowly transforming into donkeys. The long ears began to grow, then the tail, then his face changed. In the end, Pinocchio's indulgence in these vices began to weaken him so much that he morphed into a full donkey and was put into captivity by Pleasure Island's landlord.

To me, this is an impactful premise, a powerful, visual metaphor for the deceptive and destructive effects that overindulgence in sensual pleasures has on the human mind and spirit. With constant promotion of, and access to, the vices of the world at such young ages, many of our youth are living in a real-life version of Pinocchio's Pleasure Island. Constantly exposed to intoxicants, graphic imagery, sex, violence, disregard for boundaries, and disrespect for authority, the development of their mental faculties and inner moral compass is being greatly hindered.

As our generation listened to and honored the drug *dealer and pimp*, generations after us have exalted and received daily counsel from the drug *user and prostitute*. Looking at the bigger picture, neither is better than the other. In the end, dysfunction is still dysfunction.

Kickin' Knowledge And Droppin' Science

Youthful debauchery did not always reign in Hip Hop culture. Much of what we now call "gangsta rap" was once considered "reality rap" or "street knowledge." Many rappers prided themselves on the knowledge they obtained regarding culture, science, sociology and history, and sought to share their insight with their listeners. Others sought to teach and enlighten listeners about systematic oppression and choosing right action. At one time, being a knowledgeable and enlightened wordsmith was considered cool and admirable. Even those who did not necessarily focus heavily on directly educating their fans still often prided themselves on how mentally strong they were and how much class they had in the way they carried themselves.

In 2008, the cable network VH-1, which at the time was owned by media giant Viacom, compiled and aired a music video countdown, listing the top 100 greatest Hip Hop songs of all time. Public Enemy's Black Power anthem, "Fight the Power," topped the list at number one; Sugar Hill Gang's "Rapper's Delight" followed at number two; Dr. Dre's "Nuthin' but a 'G' Thang" came in at number three; Run-D.M.C. and Aerosmith's collaboration, "Walk This Way," held the number four spot; and Grandmaster Flash & The Furious

89

Five's "The Message" came in at number five. Considering that the cultural climate of much of recent "Top 40" Hip Hop has become more about excessive sex and drug use, I find it interesting that VH-1 declared two out of the top five of the greatest Hip Hop songs of all time to be socio-politically conscious songs.

Ironically, for the next two and a half decades following the 1989 hit, "Fight the Power," the Hip Hop community heard less and less music with similar socially conscious themes being promoted in the mainstream pop culture. A myth started circulating within the rap community that attempted to explain why this was happening. Simply put, it was said that the reason rappers whose music contains mostly socially conscious themes do not flood the airwaves and mainstream is because their type of music doesn't sell.

However, when looking at past sales trends of some of the Hip Hop artists who have expressed socially conscious themes, we find that, for example, albums like Eric B & Rakim's *Paid in Full* (1987) went platinum (selling at least one million units) as Boogie Down Productions' 1987 *Criminal Minded* went gold (selling five-hundred thousand units). And Public Enemy's 1988 album, *It Takes a Nation to Hold Us Back,* went platinum, while Eric B & Rakim's 1988 *Follow the Leader* went gold. This success trend continued with Boogie Productions' next three albums going gold, and Public Enemy's next album reaching platinum.

In addition, Ice Cube's first four albums and one EP, all containing heavily socio-political and economic themes, reached platinum; 2Pac's first album, *2Pacalyspse Now*, is certified platinum; the Hip Hop group Arrested Development's 1992 album, *3 Years, 5 Months and 2 Days in the Life Of...,* went four-times platinum; and Too Short's 1990 single, "The Ghetto," which offered heartfelt socio-economic commentary, is said to have sold over two million copies.

In light of these facts, the question becomes, *If Viacom – who at the time of this writing owns networks like BET, VH-1, MTV and approximately 160 other media stations – recognizes Public Enemy's 1989 song, "Fight the Power," as the greatest song in Hip Hop history, and rap artists who offered socially conscious themed music were having success in their sales, why did so-called "conscious" rap quickly start fading to the background in the immediate years to follow?*

Some say it's because the commercial success of these projects meant that more than just Black and Brown kids were throwing up their fists and chanting "Fight the Power." This means that young middle- and upper-class white youth were starting to be sympathetic and empathetic to the thoughts and struggles of the socially conscious Hip Hop community. There is much speculation about this. However, the fact remains that shortly after the resounding success of "Fight the Power," there was a shift in the common public image of the Black male rap artist. The knowledgeable and socially enlightened storyteller who was once revered in the Hip Hop community was dethroned by the ill-informed and socially degenerating wordsmith of the Crack Epidemic.

For more than 20 consistent years, the dominant, one-dimensional image of Black men in Hip Hop that was marketed to the masses became that of an excessively sexual, unforgivingly violent, drug abusing, arrogant criminal who cares about nothing but money and self-indulgence. We may conclude that even though songs like "Fight the

91

Power" reached number one on Hot Rap Singles lists and were clearly profitable, Black and Brown empowerment no longer seemed to be a message that many corporate investors wanted to continue to finance. Instead, quickly following the success of "Fight the Power" came a new dominant sound with a very different message.

In the early 1990s, prison culture and the glorification of "gangsterism" started flooding the mainstream rap industry. Teenage and young adult rappers who were openly committed to the gang and drug lifestyle rose to prominence and were promoted all across the county. I'm sure that the mass incarceration of Black and Brown youth of the time had a direct influence on creating the prison culture we find in Hip Hop and youth culture. Standing as the world's largest incarcerator of its own citizens, (as documented by the UK based International Center for Prison Studies' World Prison Population List), it's no surprise that prison culture became a significant part of American music. As I mentioned, rap music is often a very blatant reflection of values of Greater America. And though prison in itself is not necessarily an American value, the enslavement and imprisonment of Black men is.

As the popularity of gangsta rap grew, more and more corporate dollars began to be invested into projects depicting Black youth speaking explicitly about excessive casual sex, community violence and crime, and less into projects about social upliftment and community empowerment. We began to hear in the music blatant gang affiliation, true confessions of drug dealer lifestyles and more mentions of prison experiences. There became a heavy emphasis on the pleasures and personal gain that came with reckless and destructive activity while shedding very little light on the consequences that came with them.

This was the period when the "keep it real" requirement of Black rappers started to develop, and Black musical entertainers were without question required to literally live out their art or be seared and shamefully branded as "fake." This is also the time when we saw Black death packaged, marketed and sold to the world as cool and trendy American entertainment while, simultaneously, neighbor-hoods were being torn to shreds by these same realities that rappers rapped about.

It is important to note here that Hip Hop, more than any other genre, blurs the line between life and art. As youth, my generation expected our rap heroes to live what they rapped about. If they rapped about guns, we expected them to have shot somebody or been willing to shoot somebody at a moment's notice. This was such a pivotal time in Hip Hop because, as rappers were becoming very popular through sharing their semi-true stories of their lives as dope dealers, gang bangers, jackers, pimps, prison inmates and so on, their street credibility became as important as their talent and the art they produced. Contrary to popular belief, during this period we began shifting from rappers pretending to be gangstas to more gangstas pretending to be rappers.

Most young men in any neighborhood want to be cool, want to be tough, and want to have money. In the eyes of the youth, who's cooler, tougher and richer than an ex-drug-dealing, once-prison-inmate-turned-rapper who now flaunts a lifestyle of luxury on video screens across the world? Over the years, this became the social image and corresponding professional aspiration of many young American males, including myself.

It is not rap music nor so-called gangsta rap that is the problem. The rap game has given many young males, whom society had once seemed to throw away, the opportunity to be financially successful in a way that was never offered before. On the contrary, it is the lack of balance of thought amongst the most highly marketed and funded rap musicians that became the problem. While funding gun-toting, dope-selling, drug-abusing, heart-breaking, home-wrecking artist after artist, record companies began neglecting to invest in the intellectual, socially political, community driven artists. Considering that record labels probably invested in a large number of gangsta rappers who were not necessarily talented or financially profitable, we can conclude that investing in *talented* socially conscious rappers would not have presented any greater financial risks. It seems that most big record companies just weren't interested.

During the 1990s and early 2000's, the lives of rappers became the ultimate reality show. For years, Hip Hop fans were able to sit in the comfort of their own homes and listen to their favorite rapper spit about a life of crime, then watch the news and see the same rapper "keep it real" by catching a new criminal case and getting sentenced to prison, as we anticipate how the story will end. He becomes like a character in a movie.

So, why for 20-plus years has it been generally acceptable and cool to create, market and listen to song after song about the murder of young Black men and disrespecting young Black women?

The answer is simple: Because that is a value that has been accepted and upheld by our larger American society for centuries. Furthermore, that is why rappers can build prosperous careers rapping about selling dope and killing "niggas" and still get major corporate endorsements. Such themes have yet to conflict with our larger society's value system.

And it is common for people to treat others, not according to who they *are*, but according to the *image* they have accepted of them.

V. The Mis-Education Of The Educated

Product of my atmosphere,
Damaged by crack and beer,
Moving way past my fears,
We make it look attractive here.
Came here as African, chopped down to half a man
It's gonna be a long journey before me,
But I got the wind to rise again

-K-RAHN (STAR)

I'm sure at one time or another every boy, particularly in the Black and Brown communities, asks his parent or parents why he has to go to school. And when he does ask, many well-intentioned parents answer with, *"You go to school to get a good education."* The inquisitive child then asks, *"Why do I need a good education?"* To which the well-intentioned parent says, *"You need a good education to get a good job, son."*

"Well, why do I need a good job?"

"Son, you need a good job so you can make money."

At this point in the conversation, things take a turn for some of our young people. The clever son ponders to himself, "Hmm, if this whole process is about money, I can save myself eight more years of time *wasted* going to school, cut out the middlemen (teachers and employers), and start making lots of money today!" This train of thought brings us back to the entrepreneurial 13-year old kid I talked about in Chapter II, who saves up $20 to start his crack dealing business. His thought process is very logical. However, the potential moral and social consequences related to making this decision, as we now know, reveal just how very illogical such a thought process really is.

What young people of my generation and of generations to follow have realized is that, in this world, poverty is bondage and liberty is found in economics. Poverty limits access to opportunity, common comforts and one's overall quality of life. I've heard rapper KRS-1 once explain that the American mantra spoken by Patrick Henry, "Give me liberty or give me death," carries pretty much the same meaning as rapper 50 Cent's mantra, "Get Rich or Die Tryin'." The thought of the latter mantra is, "I will risk dying in an attempt to find my freedom from this victimhood and bondage of poverty."

The problem in this scenario is that many young people in heavily gang- and drug-impacted communities aren't being properly educated to discover such liberty, nor are they properly exposed to avenues and resources whereby they can adequately access healthy opportunities for economic success. Instead, they are given a one-size-fits-all-model that pushes an often false image of success to strive for. In the process, many of our youth fall by the wayside and are destroyed.

When a child asks, "Why do I have to go to school?", we should offer an honest and carefully considered answer. My own son has asked me this question. My answer was this: "Son, school does not guarantee success, but it does offer you tools you will need to gain success into adulthood. So, unless you can clearly explain to me a definite goal you have and a reasonable plan of action for creating a prosperous life for yourself that requires no formal education, then you need to go to school." This might not be the best answer, but it's the best one I got for now.

The daily plight that many urban youth face must somehow be acknowledged by the institutions responsible for their formal education. For example, practical financial literacy classes on how to earn, spend, save and invest money will help demystify finances and help students find keys to unlock the chains of economic bondage. Similarly, socially relevant critical thinking courses about how daily decision-making affects life's outcomes, are vital for counteracting the impact of growing up in communities that fail to reinforce independent, introspective, and informed thought-processing about their immediate world and the world beyond. It is also so important that such courses and their instructors be culturally competent about the communities they seek to serve.

In the height of the crack epidemic, children of the 1980s and 90s were presented with the Drug Abuse Resistance Education, or D.A.R.E., program. This was a K-12 awareness and education program that sought to prevent our country's youth from using drugs. All across the country, uniformed police officers stood in the front of classrooms, telling kids how stupid it is to use drugs. The program also included role playing activities between officers and students, in an attempt to show the class how to resist peer pressure to use drugs. Equipping students with D.A.R.E. tee shirts and an emphatic charge from our nation's First Lady at the time,

Nancy Reagan, to "Just say no," this was our country's approach to empowering gang- and drug-impacted young men and women to overcome the pressures of a drug culture that lurked throughout our neighborhoods day and night.

Cultural Relevancy

Considering the unfortunate but prevalent adversarial relationship between police and communities of color during that time, a uniformed police officer teaching urban youth about the perils of drug use was not a great idea. I'm sure some officers were effective. But even today, generally speaking, expecting or establishing immediate trust from kids growing up in such communities can still be a challenge. The D.A.R.E. program was an approach that allowed so little time with the students for relationship building that it was generally ineffective in the communities that prevention was needed the most. With that in mind, when it comes to youth engagement, a much more effective approach is to enlist, not a cop but a role model or someone with a social rapport of some sort in the kids' community who can facilitate group discussions. If the audience does not trust the messenger, then they will not trust the message. If trust is not there, then neither is there a feeling of safety. And who can learn when they feel unsafe?

I vaguely remember my experience with D.A.R.E. when I was in the fourth or fifth grade. A police officer came and spoke to our class and then gave us a white tee shirt with a green collar. On the front was a cartoon skunk and the words, "Drugs Stink." Of course, somewhere on the shirt I'm sure it also said, "Just say no."

Though in all fairness it was very nice of the officer to visit our school, the presentation had no influence on my later decisions regarding drug use. As elementary students in the 1980s, my generation was a primary target for the "Just say no" campaign. But, ironically and unfortunately, as we entered middle school and high school in the 1990s, many of us were also the crack-selling, weed-smoking juveniles that society began to refer to as *lost*.

For intervention and prevention programs to be effective, the content must first somehow respect the thought process, the groupthink and the cultural norms of the community being served, even if the facilitators do not agree with these social norms. In many urban communities, a cultural norm is to avoid law enforcement and heed the advice of older homies and entertainers who have been in the streets and understand the struggle. So, as with the D.A.R.E. program, if the content immediately honors and invites law enforcement in and disregards older homies and rappers as stupid because they have gotten involved with drug culture, then there is an immediate disconnect with the youth that the program is trying to reach. Instead, the key is for the content to skillfully identify flaws in the cultural norms, without disrespecting the culture. To disrespect the normalcy of the community is to disrespect the community, even if the cultural norm itself disrespects the community. Remember, groupthink is a powerful phenomenon.

Furthermore, the messenger of the content should be selected based on his or her credibility to share the message with the intended audience. Some call this a "license to operate," or LTO. This means the messenger not only has some form of genuine experience with the subject matter at hand but can articulate to the audience why he or she is qualified to speak to them about the subject. And then, if the intended audience accepts him or her to be the messenger, he or she may now deliver the message in a way that will be best received by the intended audience. This is important, considering that many of our young people have been voiceless and powerless in choosing their instructors within institutions.

To be truly effective in youth engagement and community crisis intervention, it is not always enough to have love in your heart and a will to work with young people. This passion and compassion should be coupled with a proper lens through which these young people are viewed and skills to engage them in their rawest, most authentic form. The program facilitator should in some way reflect the communities they choose to serve. This reflection can be shared experiences, shared values, shared ambitions, shared culture, shared identity, etc. This is to be identified by the facilitator before seeking to engage the youth. Pity and sympathy should not be the motivating factor or connection.

Seed In The Soil: The Purpose of Healthy Purpose

If we are to help our young people recognize and tap into their greatness, then a major role of general K-12 education must be to intentionally and aggressively guide their discovery of what healthy purpose each child can pursue in life beyond mundane employment for a basic income. When I mention purpose, I'm not referring to the overall, grand "cosmic plan" or why you and I were put on planet Earth to live as humans. No, I am simply referring to *a definite, personal, honorable goal in life, a reason to express determination, a motive for achieving or creating something bigger than oneself, a desirable aim or goal to strive for.*

Many people often find their purpose in their careers, in family, in a cause related to bettering their community and humanity, in religious convictions, or in artistic expression of some kind. However, when you are not properly educated or exposed to opportunities to pursue a career that interests you, and the thought of building a family of your own is dampened by the pain and dysfunction you experienced as a child, or you feel your community and humanity as a whole have turned against you, or you have not been taught or simply do not subscribe to religious convictions, and the only art you are encouraged to pursue is rap artistry or sports, what then becomes your purpose in life? What do you decide to strive for?

When looking at nature, consider how a plant typically grows. It starts as a small seed. A seed is full of potential. Generally everything a great tree is made of is contained in that tiny seed. Once watered, that seed then becomes rooted in the ground, to absorb the soil's nutrients which help it grow. Soon, when given proper sunlight and watering, it shoots above the ground. Then, with continued and consistent attention, pruning and nurturing, it flourishes into the great plant it is intended to be.

The human character and potential are similar. Our young people, as we were ourselves, are like seeds: full of potential. Full of potential to grow, evolve and transform into great and mighty beings far beyond their, and our, imagination. As with the seed, our youth must be watered – watered with knowledge and wisdom to facilitate healthy character growth, a positive self-image, strong critical thinking skills and practical tools to apply in a future profession or career.

In order for the growing child to start expanding from being a small seed, he or she needs to be rooted in proper, nutrient-rich soil. This soil represents a nurturing environment. Thoughts are often developed in response to a person's consistent environment, usually adapting to and harmonizing with it. In other words, environment feeds and shapes thoughts, and thoughts in turn feed and shape habits. Since one's environment directly influences one's life experience, it of course affects the thoughts and feelings one has about this experience and the context from which we think.

In short, our thoughts become "rooted." But what kind of soil are they rooted in? For our analogy, the "vitamins and minerals" contained in healthy soil are positive role models, insightful life experiences, positive peer to peer interactions, and regular affirmations and encouragement from within the child's immediate surrounding community. Such are the essential elements for healthy growth. When such vitamins and minerals are lacking, healthy growth is impaired.

After the seed (youth) is watered (fed worthwhile knowledge) and rooted in healthy soil (a supportive community), he or she then needs to be given adequate sunlight. Sunlight in this metaphor represents clarity of purpose. We see in nature that a plant typically grows towards the sunlight. For instance, grass and trees grow upward as they reach towards their best available source of light, the sun. Likewise, if a typical houseplant is removed from direct light and placed *near* it, over time that plant's leaves and branches will start growing in the direction towards that light.

Similarly, we as humans grow and reach towards our best available "sources of light" – that is, our purpose, our vision, our goals. And when we're not offered a positive and constructive purpose towards which to grow, we grow towards whatever purpose we feel is within reach, even if it's negative, or we don't grow at all. This is what I consider the "false light." The absence of any of these essential ingredients in the seed's life – good soil, plenty of water, and proper light – leads to the seed not properly growing into its full potential.

When seeking to engage disengaged youth, we must keep in mind that it is *purpose* that gives them *a motive (a reason to do something)*. Once purpose has been discovered, a corresponding motive/motivation arises within. It is only then that the child will become authentically *engaged* in what it is you are offering or teaching. This is the secret strength of devotion to the street organizations we call gangs. Though fear and/or the desire to belong may play a big role in gang recruitment, it is the discovery of a purpose that keeps many people, young and old, active in the lifestyle. The gang offers the new recruit an identity attached to a purpose, or cause, to live and die for.

I must note here that in helping young people find their purpose, we must be sure that it aligns with what they personally value. Many adults identify the great potential in a young person and then aggressively try to persuade them to pursue professions and careers that don't connect with who the young person really is as an individual. This can sometimes be good for the young student who moves aimlessly through life, but it can also very well lead to frustration and disappointment for both the student and the adult. Remember, just because a young person is good in math does not mean they want to be an engineer. Just because a student is extremely tall does not mean they want to be a basketball player. That is precisely why exposure to a variety of careers and professionals in those careers is essential.

Once purpose, motive/motivation and engagement have taken shape, the young person will start gaining more confidence and, in turn, reach more achievements. When someone is involved in any activity they are genuinely interested in, they feel better about themselves and feel purposeful and determined to achieve even more. This of course leads to the person's greater self-esteem and sense of self-worth.

As a result, high self-esteem indirectly leads to much more sound decision-making. When a person knows their worth, poor decisions – like hanging out and getting high all day or riding around aimlessly in a stolen vehicle with the homies – start to lose their appeal. The person recognizes the deeper, more enduring benefits of matching their decisions to their value. Subsequently, sound decisions of course open up positive opportunities, and moving forward with positive opportunities leads to a positive and successful life. It all starts with a child determining his or her definite purpose!

The opposite is true for a child or young teenager struggling with lack of purpose. When someone lacks purpose, they lack motive/motivation. Without motive/motivation, the young person won't engage in what an adult is teaching or offering even though it's positive and can change that child's life. Lack of purpose, motivation and engagement then leads to, or amplifies, lack of confidence and self-esteem. In turn, lack of confidence and low self-esteem leads to poor decision-making, which compounds lack of achievement. Poor decision-making and lack of achievement lead to a poor self-image, which leads to fear and self-sabotage. All of this leads to the lack of positive opportunities, which tragically leads to lack of success and poor life outcomes. Both the young and old need purpose!

Black Maybe

Much of the African American experience in this society has been a consistent reaction to trauma and oppression. Though this is factually the case given the historical laws, policies and practices aimed to perpetuate second-class or non-citizenship, there are still many in mainstream America who will tell this population to just "Get over it," or "It wasn't that bad" or, even more bizarre, "It never happened." To some mainstreamers, to even relate the brutal history of Black Americans to the social deficits we see today is to have what they call a "victim mentality."

Such dismissal of the African American experience fails to recognize that full U.S. citizenship for Blacks came only relatively recently, with the signing of the Civil Rights Act in 1964. It also shows ignorance about the fact that it was only about 15 years later that our communities were flooded with crack cocaine, in which we have now found out that our own U.S. government turned a blind eye. When these facts are taken into consideration, it becomes imperative for our nation to address continuing social inequities in order to rectify the social-economic, spiritual, physical, cultural and mental damage that has been inflicted upon this population for centuries.

The subject of racism can be very illusive and tricky to discuss. For one, many confuse the term "racism" with the term "prejudice." Though racism may be rooted in prejudice, it is not in itself the same. Prejudice is a pre-judging of a matter or people and refers to one's preconceived opinions that are often not based on actual experience but rather a matter of one's preconceived preference. A person may not "like" someone because of his height, gender, skin tone, accent or any other superficial attribute. However, though it may be offensive, prejudice is simply about one's attitude towards something or someone.

Though it's a fine line, racism takes this attitude further and moves it into the realm of corresponding action. Racism is about discriminating against and excluding people from human rights and fundamental freedoms of society based on race or ethnic origin. Racism often comes with lots of confusion because it is institutional and therefore often challenging to specifically pinpoint or identify. For example, just because someone makes a tasteless racial joke does not necessarily make them a racist, though they might be. I remember being in elementary school and constantly hearing jokes that started off with, "There was a Black man, a White man and an Asian man," followed by some punchline that zeroed in on common ethnic stereotypes.

It's no secret that many people are more comfortable with those with whom they share similarities, especially when it comes to cultural, identity and yes, skin color. That does not necessarily make them racist. However, purposely *excluding* and demeaning others solely based on race does. Prejudice is an attitude, racism is a practice.

America has had a tremendous facelift. Outwardly, there seems to have been massive racial progress, but behind the cosmetics is the same old gruesome reality. The United States of America was established, built and has thrived on a paradigm polluted with prejudice and racism. Though we have experienced great and positive *social* integration amongst ethnicities, the power structure of old is still very much intact and still very much segregated. This is not to say that this maintenance is always intentional. However, for centuries this nation has implemented severe and inhumane racist practices to ensure that the Caucasian population prospered far beyond that of darker skinned populations. Therefore, if the deficits that resulted from the centuries of these racist practices have not been directly addressed and rectified, then the system in place is still very much racist because it is a system that currently thrives on its momentum gained from supporting the continual prosperity of one people at the expense of another people based on the concept of race.

Let's say, for example, that we are watching a basketball game. In this game, Team A is given preferential treatment superior to that of over Team B. The referees are blatantly in favor of Team A; Team A is free to travel with the ball, double dribble and run out of bounds at will with little to no consequence, while Team B is denied such privileges and is penalized even when adhering to all the rules and regulations of the game. To make matters worse for Team B, Team A receives three points for every shot scored, while Team B receives only one point – and sometimes none, for every shot scored. As a result of this lopsided refereeing and point system, by halftime the score is 200 to 10.

At this point in the game, the officials agree that something is wrong and not completely fair. So, they decide to even the point system whereby

109

baskets scored by both teams will equal two points. However, this only applies to the second half of the game; no adjustments are made to correct the unfair deficit accrued during the first half. Also, Team A is not *as* free to violate the rules and regulations of the game without penalty as they once were, and Team B is not *as* blatantly penalized for *non*-violations. Under all of these circumstances, with the second half of the game starting at the deficit of 200 to 10, is it now equal? Does the scoreboard reflect a fair game?

Regardless, Team B must of course not wait on Team A to fully correct things but instead must continue playing the game with faith, enthusiasm, and determination.

Though many of us may not be competing for the "win" as in this somewhat overly simplified example, we do understand that our society is competitive and has certainly shown favoritism. Let's discuss a few past statistics which reveal some daunting facts about the progress, or lack thereof, of my generation and those that follow.

According to an analysis (see the following chart) released on July 26, 2011, by the Pew Research Center, the median wealth of White U.S. households in 2009 was $113,149, compared to $6,325 for Hispanics and $5,677 for Blacks. Economically speaking, these statistics do not point just to income but to wealth as it related to assets, capital and debt ratio. Income is simply the amount of money a person receives in return for his services, sale of goods, or profit from investments. Wealth is determined by the overall net worth of a person; that is, the total value of assets minus the cost of any liabilities. So, wealth is usually built cumulatively over a period of time, while income can be earned immediately.

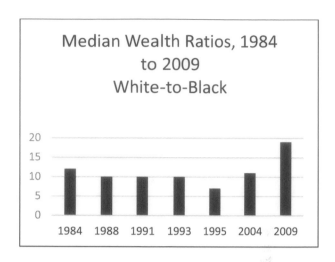

Median Wealth Ratios, 1984 to 2009 White-to-Black

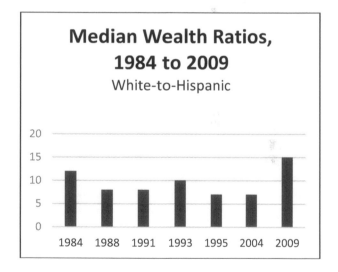

Median Wealth Ratios, 1984 to 2009 White-to-Hispanic

Notes: Blacks and Whites include Hispanics. The Survey of Income and Program Participation was redesigned for the 1996 panel. The redesign may have affected the comparability of the data from 1998 and later years with the data from earlier panels.
Sources: For 2009: Pew Research Center tabulations of Survey of Income and Program Participation data from the 2008 panel; for 1984 to 2004: various U.S. Census Bureau P-70 Current Population Reports **(PEW RESEARCH CENTER)**

This data shows that the wealth differences between White and Black households in 2009 was roughly 20-to-1, and 18-to-1 for White and Hispanics households. This means that the 200 to 10 halftime score in my basketball analogy is not hyperbole! In fact, this analysis further states that this White-to-Black wealth gap at the time was "the widest it's been since the census began tracking such data in 1984, when the ratio was roughly 12-to-1." Even more interesting, in 1995 the ratio between White and Black median wealth was 7-to-1.
(http://www.pewsocialtrends.org/2011/07/26/wealth-gaps-rise-to-record-highs-between-whites-blacks-hispanics/)

I have intentionally highlighted data from the years 2009 and 1995 because in 1995 I and my generation were teenagers. From this data, we see that the young Black man or woman who was around 15 years old in 1995 grew up in a household where the wealth gap was on average 7-to-1. Fast forward. In 2009 we see that same 15-year-old child was now approaching his or her 30s and the wealth gap was at an all-time high of 19-to-1.

So, what this indicates is that, on an economical level, it seems that my generation has been *under*-performing our parents and racial equity is moving in *reverse*. In August 2016, Tanzina Vega, CNN Money's "National Reporter for Race and Inequality," wrote, "If current trends persist, it will take 228 years for black families to accumulate the same amount of wealth as whites, according to a report released this week from the Corporation for Economic Development and the Institute for Policy Studies. For Latino families, it will take 84 years."
(http://money.cnn.com/2016/08/09/news/economy/blacks-white-wealth-gap/)

I find the amount of years Vega determines it will take for Black families to accumulate the same amount of wealth as Whites to be very ironic considering that Black people were legally held captive in chattel slavery for approximately 246 years (1619-1865).

When discussing the topic of systemic racism, many point to the success of folks like Oprah Winfrey, Tyler Perry, Michael Jordan, P. Diddy, Jay-Z and Beyonce to deny its existence. The biggest imagery they may use to support the idea that we live in a post-racial society is our former Commander-in-Chief, Barack Obama. Some say surely racism cannot exist in America if a Black man has been elected president. Twice. But what's not clear to our youth, or to those who deny current racism, is that there is a difference between the *exception* and the *norm*. These financially successful African Americans are unfortunately the exception, not the norm.

Indeed, the constant showcasing of such celebrities' wealth can cause either a great deal of inspiration or a great deal of confusion from the perspective of urban youth. Our young people grow up in a society that dangles the carrot of a lavish lifestyle while openly offering them only two routes to get there: entertainment (which includes sports) or crime. School and job security have very little relevance in this goal of becoming rich and famous. Considering the damage that has been done throughout the centuries, it seems each successive generation has had to start somewhat from scratch in regard to Black leadership, Black economic progress and Black family legacy. Unfortunately, the spoils of generational wealth in the form of money, assets, financial literacy, social status, and cultural and historical pride have gone missing. There's been

113

little warm hand-offs to current generations from those of the past.

Crack Rock Or A Jump Shot

For a lot of young people growing up in urban communities, unemployment has been consistently high, leaving many youth to accept the idea that they can't really count on traditional employment as a primary means of survival. Decade after decade, Black and Brown unemployment rates have been consistently higher than for Whites and Asians, with Blacks having the undisputed highest rate of unemployment year after year.

In this instance, my reason for mentioning these facts is not simply to focus on the rights and wrongs of racial inequality but on how its perpetuation affects the conditioning, perceptions and values of our youth. Many of our kids and young adults have never seen school or traditional employment "work" for them or their loved ones, in providing the luxurious indulgences they have been conditioned to aspire for. Therefore, when it pertains to school and traditional employment, many are left without an adequate *why*. And without the *why*, many feel little motivation to take the necessary steps towards a solid career path and financial foundation. They want jobs, but they don't count on getting them. Many of them have dreams and ambitions; but they don't understand that those dreams and ambitions are rarely ever realized with an apathetic attitude and behavior towards getting an education and developing a strong, long-term work ethic. Some may succeed without formal education, but few, if any, succeed in the long run without a strong work ethic.

I personally have found that the most important subjects in my life are spirituality, social skills and relationship building, financial literacy, health and history. Ironically, when I was coming up in the public-school system, none of these subjects was adequately taught beyond a few health lessons that mandated us to memorize the human body systems and some skewed versions of history. Of course, as I mentioned, my mother was very involved in my life and instilled great values in me. However, it was only after I left for college, which placed me in a healthy environment that supported and encouraged my character growth (fertile soil) and fed me empowering and practical knowledge (water), that I began to discover my own unique purpose (sunlight). That purpose became teaching and inspiring people around me.

Finding out the roots and history of the labels and thought patterns I once accepted as my own led me to choose *for myself* who I would be and who I would not be. I began to ask myself, *Where did my way of thinking come from? Why did I and the people before me have such disrespectful thoughts toward the men and women around me? Why did I find it so entertaining to listen to song after song about killing other Black men and abusing Black women? Why did no other race listen to songs about killing their own people and abusing their women?* Such questions had a profound effect on me. And for the first time in my life, I was sincerely excited about education.

As a high school student, I manipulated my way through much of school, using mere charm and natural talent. I saw no value in public school education toward my future and the man I was aspiring to be. While my 15- and 16-year-old peers were making hundreds or even thousands of dollars a day selling crack cocaine, tempting me to join the neighborhood business, and while other teenage friends were getting arrested and sentenced to decades of prison time for both violent and nonviolent crimes, and while my heroes flaunted across my television screen in music videos telling me how their rap career afforded them millions of dollars without obtaining a high school diploma, I was in school six and a half hours a day, daydreaming and dozing off as my teachers spoke endlessly about earth science, algebraic expressions, gerunds, participles and irrelevant reading passages. (However, I must say that somehow those 9th and 10th grade English lessons stuck with me throughout the years and actually helped me to write this book).

I often question where the social relevancy is in the daily curriculum of schools that have served heavily gang- and drug-impacted communities for decades. Where are the courses to help students navigate successfully through the tough terrain of the environment around them? Not the afterschool programs or the extra-curricular social clubs that require students to sacrifice their lunch time with friends in order to participate. I'm talking about socially relevant *life skills* and *character development* courses taught during regular school hours. Because many of our kids grow up in an environment that forces them to endure trauma on a regular basis, it would be great to see our educational institutions from coast to coast implementing curricula that acknowledge and reflect the social realities of the populations they serve. Kids must know that their reality is not being ignored, that it really matters.

Furthermore, kids must be taught how to think critically and how to excel and overcome the specific challenges they face. People see the state of much of our youth and some of the poor decisions they make and ask, "Why would that child or teenager do such a thing?" My question is, "Based on their circumstances, why *wouldn't* they do such a thing?" As I mentioned before, culture often dictates morality. If the child's surrounding culture approves of behaviors that others may frown upon, and if there has been little to no systemic approach to equip the child with the needed perspectives and resources to choose behaviors outside of the cultural norm, then why would we expect the child do anything other than what the surrounding culture accepts and promotes as good?

At the beginning of this book I mentioned a pivotal moment in my life that really effected the urgency I now have for shifting the lens of our approach to urban youth engagement. To get the full effect, let me recount it here in more detail.

I was invited by a Los Angeles mentoring organization, called See A Man, Be A Man, to speak at a high school to a small group of young men from a well-known gang- and drug-impacted community. One of the mentors was a school teacher in his mid-20s, whose class we were in; another was in his late 40s, another in his mid-50s and another in his early 60s.

As the group session began, one of the lead mentors asked the young men how their week had been. Most said "good," while a couple of them mentioned someone getting shot around the corner from their homes over the weekend. After a short dialogue, I spoke with the group about the importance of defining oneself and the need to "Live Above The Hype." The other mentors joined in as the students shared their thoughts. It was a great session.

However, what was most impactful for me about that day is what happened next. The school bell rang, indicating that class was over. The teacher/mentor expressed his gratitude, said his goodbyes and began to prepare for his next class. The other mentors and I left the classroom and began walking through the school hallway during passing period, excited about the impact we hoped we had made in those young men's lives.

As we walked and talked, a young lady around age 15 was walking towards us. She then stopped right in front of the mentor walking next to me, the one in his mid-50s who looked very healthy and was very fit and had streaks of gray in his hair. She stopped him directly in his path, looked up at him square in his eyes and asked him, "How are you old?" He stood there speechless, gave an awkward smile, looked at her, then looked at me, then looked back at her. "Excuse me?" he replied, not sure what he heard or how to answer it. With no mischievous smile or other sign of insincerity, she kept her eyes focused on his as if he was the only person in that hallway. "How are you old?" she asked him again. He continued to stand there speechless and then looked at me as if to ask if this was a rhetorical question, a joke or a genuine inquiry.

Realizing this young lady was quite serious, while thinking my wit and ability to connect with the youth would ease the awkward confusion, I looked at my puzzled colleague and smiled and then looked at this inquisitive teen. "Sista," I said, "he is old because he has been blessed to live a long life." She then shifted her stance in my direction, looked me square in the eyes and asked me an even more unexpected question, "Will I be blessed to be old?"

Now, it was I who stood there speechless and frozen, wearing the same blank stare and awkward smile on my face that my colleague just had. I think I answered, "Yes. God's will, my sista." Honestly, I'm not sure how I responded. All I know is, as the young lady began to walk away, I and the other mentors stood there silent for several moments, stunned by that brief yet incredibly impactful exchange.

What could be going on in this young lady's life, home and community where at the sight of seeing a man in his mid-50s, accompanied by three other adult male strangers, walking through her school hallway, she felt so compelled to stop him to ask, "How are you old?" She didn't ask about math or science or history. She asked how he made it to be *old*.

Her question embodied the disconnect between what many urban youth are currently being taught and what they are not being taught but should be. The community this 15-year-old child lived in has been gang-and drug-impacted and polluted with police brutality for decades. At the same time, the school she attended has been in that very same community for decades. And yet, there has been little convergence of learning and socially relevant life skills for the sake of the students' overall growth. The formal public-school education that child was receiving should in some way have spoken not only to her academic needs, but also to her immediate social development needs.

Safety First

As mentioned before, when we talk about educating urban youth, we must acknowledge and understand that our approach needs to be conducive to the severe inter-generational community traumas these communities have endured. To ignore this reality or attempt to separate it as irrelevant from the student's educational experience, immediately hinders educators' ability to properly engage heavily gang and drug impacted students. I've heard educators take pride in proclaiming that they treat all their students the same. Though I understand the sentiment, the reality is that this approach is potentially doing many of their students a disservice. All students are not the same and have different life experiences that cause them to have different needs. To offer particularly students exposed to trauma and complex trauma a cookie cutter, standardized test-driven approach will continue to cause everyone involved to fail.

Our kids need trauma-informed approaches from teachers and administrators. Indeed, just as we can see the *need* for students who are mentally or intellectually challenged or emotionally disturbed to receive "special education," our educational system must also recognize the *need* for educators serving gang and drug impacted populations to receive *specialized* education and training as well. Effective education and discipline must adapt to the learning needs and learning styles of the student. The student should not have to solely be the one to adapt to the teaching style of the instructor.

The trauma informed approach is a framework where practitioners understand, recognize and properly respond to the impact of trauma by emphasizing the six principles this framework adheres to: Safety, trust/transparency, peer support, collaboration, choice/empowerment and culture. *(https://www.samhsa.gov/nctic/trauma-interventions)*

To make these principles more practical, let's return to our previous discussion about the two young girls of "community A" and "community B" – specifically "Jackie." Remember, *Jackie*, the girl from the unsupportive community was smacked in the face, and due to her social norms, responded immediately to the situation with violence. As mentioned earlier, in issuing disciplinary action upon Jackie, she and her parents need to understand clearly that she is being treated fairly. Also, when using a trauma informed approach, the authority figure who speaks to Jackie may address the situation similar to as follows:

Safety – *"Jackie, are you ok? Would you like some water? You know the reason we do not tolerate fighting at this school is because we do not want any of you to get hurt."*

Trust – *"I can see why you fought the girl. I wouldn't want anyone hitting me either. I'm not saying it's right, but at your age, if I was in your situation I probably would have done the same thing."*

Choice/Empowerment – *"However, over the years, I've learned to think before I act and consider the consequences of my actions beforehand. I've learned that being in the right doesn't always free us from the consequences. Remember, it's in your power to choose to fight or not – but both decisions come with consequences."*

Peer support – *"In the future, if you are having problems with another student, you can always come to me or any of the other staff and we'll do the best we can to help resolve the situation"*

Culture – *"I'm not asking you to tell on your friends to try to get them in trouble. I remember being a kid, so many feel this is 'tattle-telling.' If you* *come to me beforehand, I'll do my best to make sure we address the situation without letting the students know you told us."*

Collaboration - *"I want to see you succeed. Is there any other way I, or other staff, can help you choose another way to handle situations like this different in the future?"*

(Choice/Empowerment) – *"Ok remember, I'm here to help, but the power to decide is in your hands."*

This trauma informed approach is the magical process of building relationships with young people. It is not one size fits all. It's not a checklist that needs to be considered. It's not a deep scientific process. Instead it's an approach driven by sincerity, humility and empathy.

Believe It, When I See It

Think about this. During my public-school experience, many of my peers never had one Black male teacher. With no Black or Brown male teachers or administrators, there is no one in an authority role in the entire school who resembles a young Black or Brown boy. Who is there at the school to affirm to this child's psyche that "You are welcomed here?" While other people of color are also considered minorities in mainstream culture many of them are fortunate enough to have the richness of the culture of their original homeland to draw from. In contrast, African American boys in particular usually do not have that luxury and often feel they have to rely on mainstream celebrities as relatable sources of inspiration.

According to a 2016 report by the Department of Education, titled "The State of Racial Diversity in the Educator Workforce:"

- The racial diversity of the teaching workforce can help to close the achievement gap.
- Compared with their peers, teachers of color are more likely to (1) have higher expectations of students of color (as measured by higher numbers of referrals to gifted programs); (2) confront issues of racism; (3) serve as advocates and cultural brokers; and (4) develop more trusting relationships with students, particularly those with whom they share a cultural background.
- Teachers of color are positive role models for all students in breaking down negative stereotypes and preparing students to live and work in a multiracial society.
- A more diverse teacher workforce can supplement (not replace) training in the culturally sensitive teaching practices most effective with today's student populations.
- However, 82 percent of public school teachers identified as white.

(U.S. Department of Education, Office of Planning, Evaluation and Policy Development, Policy and Program Studies Service, The State of Racial Diversity in the Educator Workforce, Washington, D.C. 2016)

It's been said that safe relationships are the greatest remedy for addressing the ill effects of trauma. However, in order to establish a safe relationship, you must sincerely *see* the other person. A safe relationship is first an *honest* relationship. You ever heard a White person say, "I

BEYOND THE CRACK GENERATION: SURVIVING A TRAUMA ORGANIZED CULTURE

don't see your color, I just see you as a human being?" I understand the intent, but then I wonder, "Why do you feel you must erase the color of my skin to see me as a human being?"

The only answer I've come up with is that the residue of white superiority remains in people's psyche. So, to say, "I don't see color, I simply see a human being" is to actually acknowledge and partially accept White superiority/Black inferiority. One doesn't have to erase the color of a car to see the vehicle as a perfectly good car, so why does one have to remove another person's obvious pigmentation from their psyche in order to see them as a fellow human?

I'm sure when the White population sees other White people, they see their color. So, what does this statement mean? What they may be well intended in saying is, "I don't see you as inferior, I see you as an equal human being and the only way I know to see you as an equal is to not acknowledge your pigmentation because I've been taught to directly correlate it with inferiority."

This point cannot be overstated. Denying my ethnicity is ignoring a huge aspect of my social experience as a human being. Despite potentially good intentions, what may also be being said is, "I choose not to acknowledge your skin color and therefore we both can ignore all the pain and social baggage that has been attached to your pigmentation for centuries and hopefully move on."

But denial is not the answer. Honesty is the answer.

A more honest, well-intentioned thought goes something like this: "Yes, I see your skin color. I acknowledge the baggage that sometimes comes with it due to prejudices and racism in our society. I acknowledge that I may or may not know what it feels like to be discriminated against. Young man or young lady, I see your tattoos and am not sure if it is gang related or simply body art. Whether it is gang affiliated or not, I accept you with little to no judgement and hope you accept me the same. I acknowledge that you may have life experiences that I am totally clueless about, which help make you who you are and which I can learn from. Yes, I see aspects of you that make me feel uncomfortable. You probably also see aspects of me that make you feel uncomfortable. I'm sure I also may have life experiences that you are totally clueless about, which help make me who I am and which you can learn from. I see you and I accept you and I hope you will do the same with me."

From my professional experience, I've observed that children learn best in the context of relationship. In attempting to engage, teach and motivate youth, it is often essential to develop a personal bond with them. Of course, these bonds must have respective boundaries. The point is, connecting with young people through humor, discussions about topics that most interest them, or guiding them to discover a goal, can help tremendously with youth engagement. That is why I feel urban youth culture sensitivity training for school staff and socially relevant curriculum for students are both necessary.

I've been asked why I often use the term "socially relevant" as opposed to "culturally relevant." To me, they are actually pretty much the same, but I intentionally use "socially relevant" to minimize confusion about the context I am referring to. I am speaking about harmonizing with the social realities of youth and the communities they live in. To say "culturally relevant" to me means the same thing because I acknowledge that our youth's culture

125

is directly related to their social realities. However, some may misinterpret my use of "culturally relevant" to mean in relation to historical ethnic culture. Though I also am in full support of historical and ethnic-centered culture being shared with our youth as well, this is not particularly what I am referring to. I know of an organization based in Los Angeles called The Village Nation that has done great work with youth in this respect.

That said, segments of school curriculum should directly address the immediate realities, desired purposes and values of the students they teach. If the entire school curriculum is of a nature foreign to the existing value system, aspirations and social realities of the student, the student will continue to be disengaged. Due perhaps to the pain, complexity and maybe even guilt attached to the waywardness of our young people, society seems to instinctually flee from confronting the growing crisis of youth disengagement. But when reflecting on my own childhood school experience, and those of many of the youth I have worked with, I find it is irrational to expect our young people to endure complex traumatic experiences on a regular basis while simultaneously being saturated with messages and images of excessive sex, drugs, materialism and violence, and then sit and focus for six hours in a classroom on a teacher or curriculum with lessons that are often irrelevant to their daily realities.

There are many teachers across our nation from diverse backgrounds who I know are developing great relationships with students, motivating, educating and engaging them in very innovative ways. These teachers care deeply, are extremely effective and work far beyond their job description. These unsung heroes should be applauded. Unfortunately, such stellar performance often relies heavily on the teacher's abundance of innate empathy and intuitive abilities to find common grounds to connect with students. It relies too heavily on the isolated pre-existing commitment, talent and perspective that individual educators bring to their profession.

My vision is to see the school system as a whole weave in such noble qualities into the very fabric of what it means to educate in order to help propel socially challenged students into academic success. I believe we are moving in the right direction. I am happy to see that the social-emotional state of students is being taken in to more consideration in education than in previous years.

Pyramids, Slave Ships And Projects

In August 1973, in Stockholm, Sweden, a famous bank robbery took place whereby the robber took four bank employees into the vault with him and held them hostage for 131 hours. By the time the employees were finally released, ironically, they had formed an emotional bond with their captor. They told reporters they now saw the police as their enemy and had developed positive feelings toward the man who once held them captive.

This psychological phenomenon later came to be called *Stockholm Syndrome,* a term coined by criminologist and psychiatrist, Nils Bejerot. It describes the irrational feelings of trust, affection or emotional attachment to a captor that a hostage forms as a result of continuous stress, dependence and a need to cooperate for survival.

In an article published on August 22, 2013, for *BBC News Magazine* titled, "What is Stockholm syndrome?", writer Kathryn Westcott quotes Dr Frank Ochberg, a psychiatrist who in the 1970s conducted extensive research on the phenomenon and defined it for governmental law enforcement agencies, the FBI and Scotland Yard. This effort was part of his work with the US National Task Force on Terrorism and Disorder to address hostage situations. According to Westcott's article, Dr. Ochberg explained the criteria for identifying Stockholm Syndrome as follows:

> *First, people would experience something terrifying that just comes at them out of the blue. They are certain they are going to die. Then they experience a type of infantilisation – where, like a child, they are unable to eat, speak or go to the toilet without permission. Small acts of kindness – such as being given food – prompt a "primitive gratitude for the gift of life." ...The hostages experience a powerful, primitive positive feeling towards their captor. They are in denial that this is the person who put them in that situation. In their mind, they think this is the person who is going to let them live. (http://www.bbc.com/news/magazine-22447726)*

I'm sure if assessed with sincerity, some form or degree of Stockholm Syndrome could apply to much of the African American population. As former kidnap victims and captives, we decide to pledge allegiance to the United States of America and in the process, honor the same forefathers who kidnapped, raped, enslaved, brutalized and dehumanized our ancestors. Past presidents whom Americans call heroes and whom we are all taught to adore, were our slave owners in previous generations, spanning for centuries. As a Black man, how can I exalt a slave owner of my people as a hero? Even if he was a so-called "nice master?" Does our resentment of him for being a slave owner mean that I have a "victim mentality" or that I do not love my country? This internal conflict is being waged inside the souls of many Black and Brown young men and women, and it's causing a moral dilemma. Do I pledge allegiance to this country, or seek rebellion? And, am I selling out if I decide to assimilate or harmonize with mainstream American culture?

Exasperating this internal conflict is the fact that mainstream society often ostracizes the people of color who do not operate by Stockholm Syndrome. For those who acknowledge the past and present atrocities inflicted upon peoples of darker skin, there is ridicule and criticism: *Why are you bringing up the past? What are you angry about? You shouldn't be protesting. If you don't like this country, just leave."*

But I often wonder if these same critics, who are so passionate about telling African Americans how we should feel and how we should react to our experience in the United States, would feel the same way about themselves if the shoe were on the other foot. If they experienced the same sufferings we historically have, would they stop acknowledging their past? Would they stop being angry about all the past and present inequalities and social ills that continue to hinder their progress? Would they refrain from any form of protest? And if they decided to protest, would they choose to only participate in protests that do not offend the very racists they are protesting against? After centuries of helping to build this country into the super power it is today through free manual labor, brilliant inventions and warfare with other lands, would they just pack up and leave because they see that changes still need to be made? And if they decided to leave, where would they go? What homeland would they claim as their own?

Self-Sabotage And Survivor's Guilt

As I stated before, no one operates beyond the boundaries of their own self-image. Therefore, we must be aware, and make our youth aware, of any self-imposed limitations that are attached to the labels our youth have accepted for themselves. These limitations become what are called *self-limiting beliefs*. *Self-limiting beliefs* are limits a person puts on themselves because of who they *think* they are or are not.

A personal example of this is when during college I was presented with the opportunity to study abroad. I had never heard of such a thing. Study abroad? What is that? Once it was explained to me that I could enroll in an academic program that would allow me to travel to another country for a designated time and continue working towards my Bachelor's degree there, I thought, *Hmm...that sounds cool. But nah. That ain't for me. That ain't what "we" do. That sounds like something "white" people do.* I quickly tossed the idea from my head, never to revisit it again for the rest of my undergraduate career. Later in life, when I looked back on this, I questioned myself. *Who is "we"? And why don't "we" do that? If travelling the world, learning and exploring different cultures "ain't something that 'we' do," then what exactly is it that "we" do?* Then I began to think, *Do I want to continue to be limited by what it is this "we" does and does not do?*

For many people of color, particularly Black Americans growing up in this trauma-organized culture, our common identity is wrapped up in our oppression and struggle. Victimhood in the form of slavery, poverty, violence, incarceration, miseducation, racism and the like becomes our common bond. Because Black Americans have been stripped of our cultural identities, languages, spiritual beliefs and connections to our historical timeline beyond the era of American chattel slavery, it is our struggle that creates a form of brotherhood. It is our recollection of ancestral oppression, coupled with today's social challenges, that indirectly unifies us.

This is a crucial point to ponder because it potentially creates confusion for us as Black people. For an individual to somewhat overcome and no longer struggle economically or academically could potentially mean they no longer "qualify" to be a part of the brotherhood, the tribe -they may no longer be considered "real." This is why it is a very dangerous irony to be defined by struggle, because it can cause some to simultaneously both pursue *and* resist the solutions to the struggle. In other words, a person is deemed to be "in love with the struggle," as some would call it, with no sincere desire for a real, meaningful resolution.

I'm sure this also has a lot to do with why many young people who grow up with this kinship to oppression may inwardly deal with self-doubt and a fear of success. Self sabotage is not exclusive to the African American community. We find people from many ethnicities and socio-economic statuses fall victim to its toxic effects. To be successful, to transition from defense to offense, can be scary. It is unknown territory – especially considering that for many young people in urban communities, triumph is the exception and not the norm. Indeed, for many growing up in environments where financial and educational lack is the norm, such triumph can easily lead to the person's isolation from the community. Add to that the fear that, at any given moment, society at large can quickly remind him or her that *"you're still a nigga."*

Where is such a person accepted? Where does he or she belong? To break through the common struggles means creating somewhat of a new identity – an identity that brings new responsibilities and new and unknown expectations. How does one comfortably and sincerely dream and aspire to accomplish things greater than those of his teachers and parents? How does one accomplish and achieve things greater than all of his loved ones without feeling some sort of guilt or other discomfort? How do I become "successful" and live a healthy and happy life while, simultaneously, still trying to continually harmonize with those who live unhealthy and unhappy lives whom I might consider unsuccessful? And how do they continue to harmonize with me? These are unspoken apprehensions some people have as they see the possibility of real success approaching. In a culture where loyalty is king and honored above all, the idea of attaining success is usually not considered worth leaving one's community, one's tribe.

The Man In The Mirror

Individual positive self-image is so important. It is crucial that we educate our youth to know that being successful is not outside of who they are. We must teach them to first define what success means to them and then how to seek to obtain it *without apology.* Faith and fear both require one to believe in something they cannot see. Faith in the positive often results in positive outcomes due to one's corresponding actions towards success. Fear of the negative often results in negative outcomes due to one's corresponding actions towards failure.

I once heard a story of a carpenter and an apprentice. The carpenter was teaching the apprentice how to drive a nail into a piece of wood. The skilled professional precisely drove nail after nail into the wood with his hammer. Holding the nail between his index finger and thumb, with a single swift strike he would hit the nail on the head, driving it completely into the wood. After watching this be done several times, the apprentice decided he was ready to try. Holding the nail between his index finger and thumb, as he saw his teacher do, he swiftly swung the hammer. Missing the nail head, the young apprentice hit his thumb. He then looked at his teacher. His teacher nodded his head and said, "Try again." The next few attempts gave the same results. Frustrated and in pain, the student asked the carpenter, "Why is it that every time you swing the hammer you hit the nail but every time I swing the hammer I hit my thumb?" The skilled carpenter smiled and said, "It's because when I swing the hammer, I focus on hitting the nail. When you swing the hammer, you focus on not hitting your thumb." Where we place our attention usually determines our outcome.

Through constant positive reinforcement, exposure to successful individuals and access to healthy environments, we must help our youth see themselves beyond struggle, oppression and the common groupthink. The focus is to shift from being content with simply surviving, to also making the necessary decisions that lead to successful life outcomes. Of course, this is no easy task. But it is an essential one.

When we understand the power of a healthy self-image, we also come to realize that fashion and coolness are attainable placebo treasures that we often resort to and exalt in order to compensate for our low self-worth and fill the immediate gaps in familial and communal acceptance and support.

For instance, we see many of our young men holding high and vivid dreams of being famous athletes. And why wouldn't they? Such dreams are safe because they are supported by the community. Likewise, failure of this dream is also supported. When a young man doesn't get drafted into a professional league, the community understands, welcomes him back home and reflects on his glory days of high school and college sports.

Have you ever encountered a child or teenager who gets an "F" on his work and thinks nothing of it? How about when he gets an "A" or a "B" and he feels amazingly surprised and proud? As a middle school teacher, I witnessed a student literally cry tears of joy when he received an "A" on a test. It was the first time he had ever received an A on a test in his life. He had grown accustomed to failure and accepted his academic failure as part of the norm. Ironically, you may hear that same kid on the basketball court yelling and playing with passion, expressing how much he hates to lose – even though his report card shows multiple losses!

In the face of such a scenario, we must ask, *where in our young people's lives are they the winner?* For some, failure is a form of rejection that they have learned to expect. It is predictable to them. They therefore, at some level, welcome this rejection because at least they know what to expect. Knowing what to expect offers them a form of safety. As adults in young people's lives, we must acknowledge that accepting failure is often just a defense or coping mechanism. We need to help their brains shift to the positive belief that success can be the norm for them, and we can do that by offering a series of opportunities for consistent small victories in their lives.

Our enthusiasm for young people's greatness must be felt by them. Sometimes, we have to believe in them more than they believe in themselves, and our belief in them must be expressed openly and constantly. It is equally important to show them instances of *their* defined success in others. A great activity is assigning them to research their ideal career or a famous role model. This is relatively easy to do with such open access to information and technology today. For those whom technology may not be as easily assessible due to lack of resources, you may suggest them visiting a school computer lab, local library or offer to print some information for them.

Explaining to youth that self-limiting beliefs are being imposed on them and that they actually have the power within themselves to reject these negative beliefs daily, can help them tremendously. It is essential that we constantly explain and reinforce the law of cause and effect as it applies to their daily lives. They must first believe that they can achieve success. Then they must know that they can only achieve their desired success if they are committed to putting in the necessary work and action steps to make it happen. We are to encourage them to constantly think critically about how each decision they make today will affect their tomorrow. One starting point is making our young people very clear about how education can benefit both their immediate and long-term lives in very practical ways.

Academics are extremely important. However, for students challenged by poor self-image, low self-esteem and allegiance to counterproductive groupthink, the role of education must extend beyond the reading, writing, arithmetic and science. Character development, critical thinking and other social skills should not be taken lightly. The mind is like a computer. It will only do what it is programmed to do. And based on our experiences, teachings and beliefs, right or wrong, win or lose, we are all programmed to do something.

People often heal *individually* by working *collectively* within a supportive community. This can be seen in substance abuse interventions and other community support-based programs. With this in mind, and in light of the fact that youth are bound by law to attend institutions such as schools and, when applicable, juvenile placement facilities and detention centers, we need to make sure such institutions are taking full advantage of the opportunity to have a positive impact on our young people. Without the implementation of socially relevant curriculum and programs in these institutions, though we may be well intentioned, we may be actually reinforcing their low self-image by indirectly telling them their reality is not important and their challenges are not worth addressing. Without cultural sensitivity in place, we are in effect telling our youth that their authentic reality has no place here.

VI. Fade To Black

I'm focused, they bogus,
my boat floating on a Lake of Fire
Fish for men with the Great Messiah
Refuse to swim with these snakes and liars.
My mind spin like Dayton wires,
From a music video at Death Row records,
It seems all of our leaders left us,
So the message is all that we're left with.

K-RAHN (SHADOWS)

The term "pop culture," or popular culture, points to what is commonly and commercially promoted in our society and what is generally accepted by the masses. Its platforms include music, advertising and marketing, movies, video games, fashion, television programming, style and so on. Over time, American pop culture has helped enlarge the human appetite for over-consumption of material gain and sensual pleasure. It has also fed and amplified the egos of both youth and adults of our society. The pursuit of happiness, seen almost exclusively in terms of personal gratification, is the norm.

In previous days, this pursuit was reserved for the rich and powerful of our country. Rich and powerful White men of old seemed to feel little to no shame in being selfish and opportunistic. In contrast, today's pop culture teaches us that this pursuit is not to be exclusive to the small power circle of men and women who rule the world. Instead, we are taught that it is the God-given privilege of even the so-called "common" man and woman to one day become rulers, kings and gods. With little to no merit, many of us feel we *deserve* to be served, we *deserve* to live in luxury and we *deserve* to have our dreams handed to us, simply because we *want* it. As a society, we search for opportunities for gain and opportunities to feed our egos, while rarely considering how our pursuits may affect others.

This is the pop culture today's young people have been nurtured in. This culture of entitlement is the pop culture that many youth of my generation were exposed to. *It's all about me! Party ova' here, F--- you ova' there!"*

In light of this, unfortunately, the curricula of much of our public-school system at best seems to disregard the influence pop culture is having on both youth culture and paradigms, and at worst feels like an attempt to suppress the undesired identity and culture of the students they serve. From personal experience, I say, such suppression leads to student resentment towards education, which of course negatively affects academic achievement.

Live Above The Hype Hip Hop Life Skills

Some people argue that adolescence is not a matter of age but instead ends when a person has developed strong social-emotional skills and is positioned for economic independence. With that in mind, as adults, parents, mentors, big homies, educators, policy makers and youth service providers, what are we offering our young people to help them transition from adolescence into adulthood? Are we properly preparing our next generation for independence in today's economic and social climate?

In 2014, I published and began teaching the first edition of a life skills curriculum called *Live Above The Hype*. At the time, this curriculum targeted academically disengaged youth and young adults in the Los Angeles area. In this course, we discuss goalsetting, community values, the state of popular music, street gang involvement, how college can help life outcomes, keys to success, drug abuse, anger management, incarceration and other socially relevant topics. Since 2014, students have told me time after time that this course helped changed their lives for the better, and even that it was the best class they have ever taken. When I ask students what they like most about it, many of them say, "I like the class because it's *real*." Some have even admitted, "I only show up to school to attend your class."

Both the young and old thirst for something *real*. That is why, in our Live Above The Hype class sessions, students are assigned academic lessons about various subjects that directly relate to their immediate reality. In a non-judgmental way, we have class discussions about selected reading followed by writing assignments that require students to think critically about their personal paradigms as it relates to "pop culture." As a result, these lesson plans usually keep students intrigued and eager throughout the curriculum.

Moreover, the Live Above The Hype curriculum allows everyone in the room to be both teacher and student. I, as the facilitator, take the lead and often share my personal experiences of triumph, failure, fear, ignorance, dysfunction and redemption. My transparency helps to create a safe environment where students feel their true identity is welcomed. Together, we discuss our insecurities and struggles and ways to overcome them, work to define success and self-evaluate our daily decisions, and determine if these decisions are pulling us toward our success or pushing us away from it. We're honest about both the allures and the detriments of street life, unproductivity and wasteful living.

The intent of the Live Above The Hype curriculum is not to tell students how bad they are, how bad their decisions are or how bad their surrounding culture is. Instead, it is designed to guide them and to help them develop their critical thinking skills so that they can assess their own lives and come up with sound conclusions for themselves in regards to what they truly want in life. We don't teach them *what* to think; we teach them *how* to think. Addressing the source of much of our youth's problematic behavior, the curriculum speaks directly to the culture, mindset and value system that our students are potentially living in and teaches them to think ahead and make meaningful, proactive choices that will positively impact the success of their life.

Faith

As adults work in the lives of youth, we must remember that each young man and young woman we encounter has their own unique journey to walk. We are not the ones who get to decide what is a suitable path for each of them to take. We are simply guide posts to help them along their way. In our education, intervention and prevention services, though we may be responsible for the *process*, we do not own the *outcome*. We may plant, water and shine light on the young seeds that come into our lives, but we can't make the grass grow. That is not our position.

The work we do requires devotion and faith. We must trust that our individual purposes in being involved in their lives are best fulfilled by doing our best to serve them and guide them on their path. We may not have the privilege of seeing the positive outcome. The transformation may not reveal itself the way we hoped it would or when we hoped it would. But, with every seed we plant, we have to believe there will be a harvest. My mother had many sleepless nights worrying about me, questioning why I was making the decisions I was making. My college counselor never saw how much I had evolved during my college experience. The authors of the books I read have no idea how their written words changed my life. They all simply offered their best and trusted that it would bring about the positive results they purposed.

Furthermore, in working with our young people, though I acknowledge the challenges many must face, I do not hold to the "oh poor little, unfortunate child who is subjected to such horrible living conditions" perspective. Misplaced sympathy can be extremely offensive because it is condescending. Our young people do not need pity. They instead need empathy. Especially if we are outside observers to their community, regardless of whether we personally find their social conditions undesirable, we must acknowledge and honor the fact that, to the young people we work with, this is *home*. And it is home, not only to them, but also to many great people whom they love and honor. Many well-meaning people claim to be nonjudgmental. However, having a low perception of, or presuming low standards and expectations upon, the population we serve simply because of their social environment, is judging.

It is a crucial yet delicate skill to be aware of all of the factors we have discussed in this book while still being open to the fact that not all of our young people who grow up in these environments have the same experience. Some of these kids come from two-parent households, some have parents who are professionals, some have never been involved in crime, some do not like rap music, some have no desire to experiment with drugs or join a gang, and some are academically excelling and are crystal clear about their purpose.

Furthermore, I do not seek to *save* our youth. Instead, I seek to offer guidance where I can, to those who need it and are open to it. I focus on helping our young people heal. If they are "delivered" from destruction in the process, I offer gratitude to God for the redemption as I continue in my own purpose and soul mission. In staying committed to doing all I can do and having faith that my contribution is enough to effectively complete my divine assignment in a person's life, I am at peace with both myself and the outcomes.

I understand that one's environment and experiences have a direct effect on their social and emotional states and self-image. I realize that one's social and emotional states have an effect on their values, and that one's values have an effect on their behavior. Therefore, I acknowledge that this work is much bigger than me. I choose not to make the mistake of simply addressing the behavior of our so-called "at-risk" youth without tapping into the values and paradigms in which their behavior is rooted. The dysfunction we see in much of our youth is simply a normal perpetuation of the dysfunction that our greater society cultivates around them.

Unfortunately, many public-school educators and youth service providers, while no fault of their own, have not been properly informed on and trained to effectively engage their students who grow up in these social realities. That is why, during the Urban Youth Culture Competency & Engagement Training™ that I offer, mostly to professionals working with heavily gang- and drug-impacted youth, we acknowledge and address the fact that youth engagement begins with understanding youth paradigms. As I've said, and it cannot be emphasized enough, one of the most effective ways to motivate a person is to engage in what that person values.

My generation did not create the social conditions or value systems in which we were raised, nor did our children. As adults and professionals, many of us ourselves have trauma-organized habits that we have not yet overcome. Our development as citizens has been so deeply influenced by generations of trauma that I doubt any of us really has a clear idea of what healthy behavior looks like, or how it truly feels to live in a healthy society, or what is truly necessary to create and maintain one. In the meantime, I am encouraged by these words from psychiatrist Bruce Perry: "There is no more effective neurobiological intervention than a safe relationship." So, while Hip Hop has been blamed as the source of the problems relating to our youth, we may now discover that understanding the culture and the paradigms associated with it may in fact be a huge part of the solution.

Peace. Power. Light.

Made in United States
Orlando, FL
04 April 2022